Financial Help for Families

What you need to know

Child Poverty Action Group

Published by Child Poverty Action Group
30 Micawber Street
London N1 7TB
Tel: 020 7837 7979
info@cpag.org.uk
cpag.org.uk

A CIP record for this book is available from the British Library.
ISBN: 978 1 915324 27 6

Child Poverty Action Group is a charity registered in England and Wales (registration number 294841) and in Scotland (registration number SC039339), and is a company limited by guarantee, registered in England (registration number 1993854). VAT number: 690 808117

Cover design by Colorido Studios
Internal design by Devious Designs
Typeset by DLxml, a division of RefineCatch Limited, Bungay, Suffolk
Content management system by KonnectSoft
Printed and bound in the UK by CPI Group (UK) Ltd, Croydon CR0 4YY

Note: the benefit rates in this book are those that apply in 2025/26 and may change in future years.

Author

Mark Willis is a welfare rights worker at CPAG in Scotland.

Acknowledgements

Many thanks are due to Alison Gillies, Trevene Highfield, Maria Marshall, Rosie Mears, Simon Osborne, Owen Polley, Jo Porter, Fran Ryan, Owen Stevens, Jessica Strode, Ruby Sullivan and Katie Wood. Also, with thanks to Pauline Phillips for managing the book's production, Anne Ketley for compiling the index and Kathleen Armstrong for proofreading the text.

About Child Poverty Action Group

Child Poverty Action Group is a national charity that works on behalf of the more than one in four children in the UK growing up in poverty. We use our understanding of what causes poverty and the impact it has on children's lives to campaign for policies that will prevent and solve poverty – for good.

We provide trusted and expert information and advice for the welfare rights and advice community – online, and through our books, training and advice services. Our advice lines support thousands of advisers a year, helping them to give families the best information and advice. Our *Welfare Benefits Handbook*, described as the 'adviser's bible', is used by Citizens Advice, local authorities and law centres throughout the UK. We also keep advisers up to date with trends and changes in the social security system through bulletins and our highly regarded training courses and seminars.

Poverty affects more than one in four children in the UK today. When children grow up poor, they miss out – and so do the rest of us. They miss out on the things most children take for granted: warm clothes, school trips, having friends over for tea. They are likely to do less well at school and earn less as adults. Any family can fall on hard times and find it difficult to make ends meet. But poverty is not inevitable. With the right policies every child can have the opportunity to do well in life, and we all share the rewards of having a stronger economy and a healthier, fairer society.

If you would like to join us to help end child poverty, please visit cpag.org.uk, or follow us on Facebook (facebook.com/cpaguk) and X (@cpaguk).

Keeping up to date

Advisers can get the latest information on benefits by booking on a CPAG training course. We can also provide your workplace with in-house training. See cpag.org.uk/training for more information.

Our *Welfare Benefits Handbook*, published every April, tells you all you need to know about entitlement to benefits and other payments.

With up-to-date information, insights, decision-making tools and appeal-letter generators, CPAG Welfare Rights is our online platform that supplements the expertise advisers have come to trust and rely on from our rights handbooks and training. CPAG Welfare Rights provides digital access to our flagship *Welfare Benefits Handbook*, which is fully searchable and updated throughout the year online. See cpag.org.uk/subscriptions to subscribe or find out more.

Universal credit Early Warning System

CPAG's Early Warning System collects and analyses information about the impact of the roll-out of universal credit, as well as other changes in the benefits system. The cases we hear about inform our legal challenges, policy and campaign work. You can submit case studies or read our findings at cpag.org.uk/early-warning-system.

Getting advice

Your local Citizens Advice or other advice centre can give you advice and support on benefits. See citizensadvice.org.uk if you live in England or Wales, or cas.org.uk if you live in Scotland.

CPAG has an advice line for advisers. If you can't hear or speak on the phone, you can contact the advice line using Relay UK.

For advisers in the UK:
Telephone: 020 7812 5231, Monday to Friday 10am to 12pm and 2pm to 4pm.
Email: advice@cpag.org.uk (for enquiries about universal credit and child benefit only).

For advisers in Scotland:
Telephone: 0141 552 0552, Monday to Thursday 10am to 4pm and Friday 10am to 12pm.
Email: advice@cpagscotland.org.uk.

Contents

Throughout the book, the Department for Work and Pensions is referred to as the DWP.

Chapter 1
Support for families

This chapter covers:

1. **Why are families struggling for money?**
2. **What financial support is out there?**
3. **What does this guide cover?**
4. **Working with families**

What you need to know

- Many people do not get all the financial support to which they are entitled.
- Getting a benefit check, and advice about challenging benefit decisions, can make a real difference to household income.
- Debt, energy, budgeting and housing advice can also help people to make ends meet.
- If you work with a family with money worries, there are lots of ways you can support them, including by referring them for the support and advice they need.

1. Why are families struggling for money?

More than one in four children in the UK are living in poverty. For parents, this means not having enough money to buy essentials and sometimes having to make difficult choices between buying food for the family and paying bills.

Some parents struggle for money because they are not able to work, or they work fewer hours than they would like, or their wages are low.

High costs of housing, food, fuel and childcare also make it harder to manage. Benefit rates have not kept up with the rising cost of living over the last decade. Meanwhile, benefits policies such as the two-child limit and the benefit cap have strictly limited many parents' incomes. So for many families who get a social security benefit, it is harder than before to make ends meet.

What families say

Making ends meet

'Since we had our youngest and didn't get any extra money because of the 2 child limit, I have to cover the cost of formula and nappies with no extra money. I have to budget carefully to get enough food for all the children and both adults. I have a journal where I write down all my monthly bills... I try and forget about myself and just make sure everyone else is fed, and then I just eat whatever I can afterwards.' *Young mum of four, Early Warning System*

'I've just got through the bank holiday and I feel bad that my 2 children are cooped up inside the house but if I go out that costs money that I don't have.' *Faith N, Changing Realities*

Benefits are available to help most families, but many people do not know what they are entitled to. When people do claim benefits, some experience delays, incorrect decisions, reduced payments and other problems.

Some families are hit harder than others by recent changes in the benefits system. Throughout this book we have included some real-life examples from CPAG's Early Warning System project, which was set up to monitor and analyse the impact of the changes on children and their families. Other examples are from Changing Realities, a partnership between parents and carers, the University of York and and CPAG that is documenting and working to change life on a low income.

- **Lone-parent families**. Almost half of children living with one parent live in poverty – nearly twice the rate of children living with two parents. Lone parents are more likely than two-parent families to claim benefits (since they are likely to have a lower household income from work) and benefits are likely to make up a higher proportion of their overall income.

- **Families with more than two children**. Universal credit includes amounts for children, but not usually for a child born after 6 April 2017 if two children are already in the family. Larger families can also have their universal credit reduced due to the benefit cap, regardless of when their children were born. So families with three or more children may struggle for money.

Box A
Changing Realities

Changing Realities is a participatory online project working with more than 200 parents and carers living on a low income across the UK. By sharing experiences of life on a low income across a range of platforms, the project aims to engage the public, media and government to drive much-needed change. Changing Realities is a collaboration between parents and carers, researchers at the University of York, and CPAG. You can find out more at changingrealities.org.

2. What financial support is out there?

There are three main kinds of benefits.

- **Means-tested benefits to help with living costs** if you are out of work or if you are in work but have a low income. Whether you qualify and how much you get depends on your income and savings. The amount you get is also often affected by the size of your family, your and your children's health, and whether you are a carer. The main means-tested benefit is universal credit, or pension credit if you and your partner are over pension age.
- **Non-means-tested benefits to help with living costs in particular circumstances**. These circumstances include bereavement, being a

carer or stopping work due to illness. You can usually get this kind of benefit regardless of your income or savings, although sometimes there are rules about maximum earnings. There can also be other conditions for eligibility – eg, payment of national insurance contributions. Examples include carer's allowance and bereavement support payment.

- **Non-means-tested benefits to help with extra costs**, such as the costs of having a disability or having a child. The amount you get does not depend on how much income or savings you have. Examples of extra-costs benefits include child benefit and personal independence payment.

You can often get more than one benefit at once – eg, you could get a disability benefit and child benefit, plus a means-tested benefit to help with living costs. You can ask a local advice agency for a benefit check to find out what you might be entitled to. If you are already claiming a benefit, you can check whether you are getting the right amount and if you are eligible for any other benefits. Even a small amount of universal credit is worth claiming, for instance, because it may help you qualify for other financial support.

EXAMPLE

Claiming universal credit

Emily is a lone parent of school-aged children. She works and gets child benefit. She gets a benefit check at her local advice centre. The adviser tells her that she could also get a small amount of universal credit each month. If she starts to receive universal credit, she can qualify for the Warm Home Discount of £150 off her annual bill from her energy supplier.

In addition to benefits, there are lots of other sources of financial help that depend on your location and circumstances – eg, council tax reduction schemes and local welfare assistance schemes.

There are some different benefits in Scotland.

Box B

Residence and immigration conditions

Most of the financial help described in this guide depends on meeting certain residence and immigration conditions. These conditions can affect claimants and family members who have come to live in the UK from another country, including British citizens who have been living abroad. The rules are different for different benefits, and can be complex.

Generally, British and Irish citizens, people with indefinite leave to remain (settled status), refugee status or humanitarian protection are entitled to claim benefits under the usual rules. People with no recourse to public funds are excluded from most benefits as a condition of their permission to be in the UK, but may qualify for some benefits such as maternity allowance. Asylum seekers are excluded from benefits and receive support from the Home Office instead. European nationals with pre-settled status may qualify for benefits but need to meet additional tests.

Chapter 12 lists the eligibility conditions for each benefit, including any immigration restrictions (and with terms explained in the glossary). If you are supporting a family to access financial help, you should always check whether they are affected by these rules and, if their immigration status is not clear, seek further advice from specialist services.

What can you do if you have a benefit problem?

Problems do sometimes happen. You might be wrongly told that you cannot get a benefit, or be paid an incorrect amount. Your benefit could be reduced by deductions to repay debts or overpayments. Your benefit could be reduced due to a sanction if you have not met your work-related requirements. Benefits are set at a minimal amount intended to live on, so this will leave you without enough money to get by. You might not get enough help to pay your rent, because of rules like the bedroom tax or benefit cap. Whatever the problem, it is best to get advice quickly from a local advice service. An adviser can give you practical advice, can help you appeal and may be able to suggest other sources of financial support. There is a very good success rate with benefit appeals, so it is well worth appealing if you can. Chapter 11 has more information on challenging decisions.

3. What does this guide cover?

This guide covers all the main social security benefits that you may be able to get for you and your family. It covers benefits available throughout the UK as well as different payments only available in Scotland. It also covers other important financial support, such as child maintenance and help with childcare costs. You can use this guide to find out:

- which benefits you can get when you are having a baby
- how to apply for child maintenance and how much you might get
- whether you can get free childcare or help with childcare costs
- how to get help with school costs, such as clothing, meals and transport
- which benefits you can get if you are out of work or if you have a low income from work
- what you might be expected to do to get ready for work as your children get older
- how benefits can help with your rent or mortgage
- what help is available if someone in the family has a disability
- which benefits to claim after a bereavement
- how benefits are affected if a child goes into care
- the benefits available for foster carers and kinship carers
- what financial help is available if you have experienced domestic abuse
- how to deal with benefit problems
- what financial help is available in an emergency

When you have identified the help that is available in your circumstances, you can find out more about eligibility, how to claim and how much you will get in the A to Z list of social security benefits in Chapter 12.

4. Working with families

Talking about money and debt

Our research shows that parents are often anxious about telling people that they have money worries, which may mean they do not seek help and support. A family may be more likely to open up to someone they are used to working with and trust, rather than someone they have never met before. This is why it is important that everyone who works with families feels confident asking about money worries and can help families make contact with the help and support they need. You do not have to be a benefit expert to do this.

Thinking ahead about how you will raise the subject will help you to do it confidently.

Be alert for things that your client says that may indicate possible money worries, and make asking about money worries part of your routine enquiries. That way, you avoid singling out people who may consider there is a stigma attached to being assessed by a professional. It also makes sure you do not miss anyone who might benefit from advice.

Ask opening questions, such as:

- 'Children can be so expensive. Do you find it difficult to make ends meet?'
- 'Do you have any debt?'

Using positive language, reassure your client that help is available:

- 'Advice services can check that you are getting all the benefits you are entitled to.'
- 'Benefit decisions can be wrong. Advice services could double check that decision for you and support you to challenge it if need be.'

Once you have asked your client about their money worries, you need to help them get the advice and support they need.

Signposting means you give your client details of an advice service, for them to get in touch with the service directly.

A referral means that you contact the advice service and start the process of making an appointment.

Clients are much more likely to engage with an advice service following a referral than if they have to make contact with the advice service themselves. You will need to be aware of the local advice and support agencies.

Developing a good-quality referral system between your service and advice services improves access to quality advice and support, which can help maximise families' incomes and prevent or alleviate financial crisis. A 'gold standard' referral system would be universal, or near universal, allowing referrals for anyone who has a low income or money worries of any kind. In addition, it would not rely on action from the parent – the appointment with the advice service would be made as part of the referral, and if this were not possible the parent would be contacted directly by the advice service to make an appointment.

Practical action you can take

Depending on your job role, you might be able to help your client with many of the following actions.

- Referring your client for a benefit check. This can make a real difference. For example, many people getting universal credit are missing out on extra elements related to their or their children's health.
- Referring your client for an energy check. This could reduce the amount the family is spending on energy bills.
- Helping families deal with debt. Debt advice could reduce the amount the household is spending on debt repayments, and budgeting advice could prevent a family from getting into debt in the first place.
- Making an application for emergency financial support (known as local welfare assistance) from the local authority.

- Contacting the relevant agencies about your client's benefits. You must have your client's consent to do this, and details such as their national insurance number. You may be able to help sort out some things over the phone while your client is with you, but you need their written consent for further involvement.
- Accessing and using equipment, setting up an email address or opening a bank account, which are needed to claim benefits online.
- Asking for a benefit advance while waiting for their first payment.
- Asking for a benefit decision to be looked at again. If someone thinks that a benefit decision is wrong, they can ask for it to be looked at again within one month of the decision. In some circumstances, a late request can be accepted within 13 months – eg, if they have a good reason for not having asked earlier.
- Applying for a discretionary housing payment. Local authorities can make discretionary payments to people receiving universal credit or housing benefit if their benefits do not cover all of their rent.
- Helping your client to avoid a sanction by making sure the job centre knows about the things that will affect their ability to look for work – eg, their health or childcare responsibilities.
- Asking for a sanction to be looked at again. If someone has been sanctioned but thinks that the decision is wrong, they can ask for it to be looked at again – eg, because they had a good reason for not doing what was asked of them.
- Asking for a hardship payment from the DWP to help somebody get by while they are sanctioned.
- Referring for specialist welfare rights advice if the issue is more complicated, such as a fraud allegation or needing representation at an appeal tribunal. It will help if you can obtain details about which benefit and the date of any decision.

Making your service accessible to families

It is worth taking time to consider whether there is more you could do to make your service accessible and useful to families living on a low income, such as the following.

- Is there a freephone number?
- Could you pay travel costs in advance?
- Do the location and opening times for your service mean it is accessible by public transport?
- Are there hidden costs attached to using your service? For example, if you provide free childcare, are families expected to cover the costs of snacks or outings?
- Do you have links with local advice services? Could you improve these links and develop pathways to directly refer families?
- Do staff know about sources of emergency financial support?

Further information

Finding an advice service
As a starting point, you can find services offering advice on benefits, debt and housing by entering your postcode at advicelocal.uk

Benefit checks or support to ask for a decision to be looked at again
You can find your local Citizens Advice office at citizensadvice.org.uk – they can also help with debt, employment, housing and energy advice.
Some local authorities have their own welfare rights service. Check on your local authority website.
Many housing associations have a welfare rights service for their tenants.
Online benefit calculators can give you an idea of what benefits you could get: gov.uk/benefits-calculators

Questions about benefits
CPAG provides advice to frontline staff working with the public.
In England, Wales and Northern Ireland: 020 7812 5231 or advice@cpag.org.uk (email advice is limited to queries about universal credit and child benefit)
In Scotland: 0141 552 0552 or advice@cpagscotland.org.uk for all benefit queries, including Scottish payments

Energy check
The Energy Saving Trust: energysavingtrust.org.uk/about-us/contact-us

Debt advice
National Debtline: 0808 808 4000 and nationaldebtline.org
StepChange: 0800 138 1111 and stepchange.org.

Housing advice
Shelter helpline: 0808 800 4444; Wales: 08000 495 495. You can also find online advice and a webchat service at england.shelter.org.uk/get_help or scotland.shelter.org.uk/get_help or sheltercymru.org.uk/get-help

Who to contact about different benefits
See Chapter 12 for more details
For Scottish benefits, you can also call 0800 182 2222 or chat to a client adviser at chat.socialsecurity.gov.scot

Chapter 2

Having a baby

This chapter covers:

1. What help is available?
2. What help can you get while you are pregnant?
3. How are your benefits affected if you are pregnant?
4. What help can you get when your baby is born?
5. Are you a young parent?
6. Are you adopting a child?
7. Are you taking on responsibility for a child in other circumstances?

What you need to know

- Find out about support to which you are entitled – get a benefit check as soon as possible after you become pregnant, and again once your baby is born.
- Tell your employer or your work coach at the job centre that you are pregnant.
- Make sure you know your rights at work.
- If you are a young parent, find out whether you can claim or whether your family can claim for you.
- If you are adopting a child, you can qualify for the same, or similar, financial help.

1. What help is available?

Among all the things to consider when you are having a baby, money is likely to be high on the list. Your maternity period is a time when you may have a reduction in income if you are in work, and an increase in spending, whether you are in work or not. There are some payments and financial help available to you in these circumstances to support you, and help you prepare and provide for your new baby.

Box A

Financial help if you are having a baby: checklist

- free vitamins
- Healthy Start scheme, or Best Start foods in Scotland
- Sure Start maternity grant, or Best Start grant in Scotland
- help with NHS costs
- statutory maternity pay
- statutory paternity pay
- statutory shared parental pay
- statutory neonatal care pay
- maternity allowance
- statutory adoption pay
- universal credit
- child benefit
- Scottish child payment (if you live in Scotland)

2. What help can you get while you are pregnant?

When you find out you are pregnant, it is worth getting a benefit check as soon as possible to make sure that you do not miss out on anything you may be entitled to. Your GP, health visitor or midwife may be able to refer you to a local advice agency.

Being pregnant, at least in the early stages, may not make any immediate difference to your financial circumstances. You are not automatically entitled to any additional cash payments just because you are pregnant; the financial help available depends on your income, age and work history.

Universal credit

You may be entitled to universal credit during pregnancy. This can include an amount for yourself and for housing costs. The amount depends on whether you have other income or savings. If you live with your partner, you must claim as a couple and the amount depends on joint income and savings. You must usually be aged at least 18. If you are 16 or 17, you can qualify from 11 weeks before your due date, or at any time if you are 16 or 17 and without parental support. You must usually not be in education, but you can get universal credit as a student when you are responsible for a child (but not during pregnancy), or if you are disabled, or if your partner is not a student. You can also qualify for universal credit as a student if you are in non-advanced education, under 22 and without parental support (including during pregnancy).

Free vitamins

If you live in Scotland (and in some health authorities in England and Wales), you can get free vitamins during your pregnancy. These are provided to all pregnant women, regardless of their income. Ask your GP or midwife. In other areas, you can get free vitamins if you qualify under the Healthy Start scheme.

Healthy Start scheme and vitamins

The Healthy Start scheme in England, Wales and Northern Ireland can help towards your food shopping to pay for milk, fruit, vegetables and pulses (see Box B). You can get £4.25 a week during pregnancy, £8.50 a week per child aged under one and £4.25 a week per child aged one to three. You can use the payment card at shops that sell the eligible Healthy Start food items and accept Mastercard.

The scheme also provides free vitamins during pregnancy and your baby's first year, and for children. You can qualify for the scheme from when you are 10 weeks pregnant and until your child's fourth birthday. Healthy Start children's vitamins are for children aged from six months old or who are having less than 500ml (one pint) of infant formula a day. Babies under six months old who are fully breastfed might benefit from them earlier – ask your midwife or health visitor for advice.

If you are under 18 and pregnant, you qualify for the Healthy Start payment card and vitamins, regardless of your income.

If you are aged 18 or over, you can qualify if you or your partner are entitled to any of the following benefits:

- universal credit (provided your and your partner's combined earned income is no more than £408 a month)
- income-related employment and support allowance during pregnancy
- pension credit

Your qualifying benefit will be checked with the DWP. It is your responsibility to report any changes in your circumstances.

You can also qualify if you have no recourse to public funds due to your immigration status and are responsible for a child under four who is a British citizen, and your family earns £408 a month or less.

Box B

What can you spend your Healthy Start or Best Start foods payment card on?

The payment card can be used for milk, fruit, vegetables and pulses (and, for Best Start, eggs).

Milk must be plain cow's milk and can be whole, semi-skimmed or skimmed. It must also be pasteurised, sterilised, long-life or ultra-heat treated (UHT), or infant formula milk suitable from birth. You cannot spend your payment on flavoured milk, coloured milk, evaporated milk, condensed milk, goat's milk, soya milk, vitamin-enriched milk or other powdered milk.

Fruit and vegetables must be fresh, frozen or canned, with nothing added to them, such as fat, salt, sugar or flavourings.

Pulses, such as beans, lentils and chickpeas, can be fresh, dried or canned, with no added fat, salt, sugar or flavourings.

You can qualify for the Healthy Start payment card and free vitamins once you are 10 weeks pregnant, so it is worth applying around this date because your entitlement cannot be backdated to a date before you applied. You do not have to wait for an ultrasound scan. The payment card is credited every four weeks, but any money you do not spend remains on the card balance and can be used in future.

Best Start foods

The Best Start foods payment card in Scotland can help towards your food shopping. Best Start foods payment cards are credited every four weeks, to the value of £5.40 a week during pregnancy, £10.80 a week per child aged under one and £5.40 a week per child aged one or two. You can use the card at all major supermarkets and smaller local shops that accept Mastercard. You can spend it on milk, fruit, vegetables, pulses and eggs (see Box B). If you qualify for Best Start foods, you should also be able to get free vitamins from your health board. You can qualify for Best Start foods from the start of your pregnancy until your child's third birthday.

If you are under 18, or 18 or 19 and a dependant, you qualify for Best Start foods regardless of your income. You continue to qualify until the end of your pregnancy if you turn 18, or are no longer a dependant 18/19-year-old, while pregnant. You continue to qualify until your child's first birthday if you turn 18, or are no longer a dependant 18/19-year-old, after your baby is born. You are a dependant 18/19-year-old for as long as someone else is responsible for you for child benefit, universal credit or pension credit.

If you are aged 18 or over, you qualify for Best Start foods if you or your partner are entitled to any of the following qualifying benefits:

- universal credit
- income-related employment and support allowance
- pension credit
- housing benefit

If you stop getting a qualifying benefit, you continue to qualify for Best Start foods for eight weeks. You can also qualify if you have no recourse to public funds due to your immigration status and are responsible for a child under three, and your monthly income is £1,792.71 or less as a single person, or £2,121.02 or less as a couple (after tax).

You can apply as soon as you find out you are pregnant, and are not required to provide evidence of pregnancy until around 24 weeks, when you are offered a baby box.

Box C
Baby boxes in Scotland

The Scottish government offers a free baby box to all new parents in Scotland, regardless of their income. Some hospital trusts in England and Wales have also introduced baby boxes. The box, which is suitable for your baby to sleep in, contains basic items worth more than £200 including clothing, a changing mat, mattress, thermometer, play mat and books.

See parentclub.scot/baby-box for more information.

Sure Start maternity grant

The Sure Start maternity grant in England and Wales provides help with the costs of pregnancy or a new baby (usually only your first baby) if you are on a low income. If you qualify, you are paid £500 in a lump sum into your bank account. You do not need to repay it. You can spend the money on whatever you think you and your baby need most, and you do not have to provide evidence of what you have spent it on.

You may qualify for a Sure Start maternity grant if you are pregnant or have given birth in the last six months, and you or your partner are entitled to any of the following qualifying benefits:

- universal credit
- income-related employment and support allowance
- pension credit

You cannot usually get a Sure Start maternity grant if there is another child under the age of 16 in your family, even if you have not received a grant before or if the other child is not your birth child. However, there are exceptions to this rule:

- for multiple births
- if the other child in your family was over 12 months old when you became responsible for them
- if you have your first baby while you are under 20 and you are part of someone else's benefit claim
- if you are a refugee or are in the UK under schemes for Afghan or Ukrainian nationals, and your older child was born before you came to the UK

If you have a multiple birth and have no other children, you can get a grant of £500 for each baby. If you have a multiple birth and have older children, you can still get a grant but not one for each baby. The number of grants payable is reduced by the number of other children you have from a single pregnancy.

EXAMPLES

Multiple births

Olivia gives birth to twins. She has no other children. She is entitled to two Sure Start maternity grants.

Dabeer has one child, aged three, and then has twins. She is entitled to one Sure Start maternity grant for the twins.

Eve has twins aged three, and then has another set of twins. She is not entitled to a Sure Start maternity grant for the new twins.

If you have a baby when you are under 16, or under 20 and in full-time non-advanced education (eg, you are at school or college studying for GCSEs or A levels) and you are included in someone else's benefit claim, that person can claim a Sure Start maternity grant for your baby, even if there are other children aged under 16 in the family. They must be getting universal credit (or pension credit) and this must be your first baby.

EXAMPLE

Under 20 years old

Hayley is 16 and at school. She is pregnant. Her mum, Clare, gets universal credit, which includes an amount for Hayley, as well as for Hayley's brother and sister, aged 12 and 14. Clare can claim a Sure Start maternity grant for Hayley's baby, even though there are other children aged under 16 in the family.

You can claim a Sure Start maternity grant from 11 weeks before the date your baby is due, and within six months of the birth. If you do not claim within six months, it cannot be paid under any circumstances. The date of your claim is usually the date the completed form is received by the DWP.

If your child is born alive at any stage of pregnancy and dies or is stillborn after 24 weeks of pregnancy, a grant is still payable, and does not have to be repaid. Chapter 8 has more information on financial help that is available if your child dies.

If you or your partner are waiting to hear about whether you are entitled to universal credit (or pension credit), do not delay claiming a Sure Start maternity grant. A decision may be put on hold or, if your claim is turned down, you can claim again once universal credit (or pension credit) is awarded.

Best Start grant

The Best Start grant in Scotland consists of a payment to help with the costs of pregnancy or a new baby, and two more payments in the early years. The pregnancy and baby payment is £767.50 for your first baby, or £383.75 if you have another child aged under 16 in your household. The higher amount is still payable if the other child is:

- a parent of the baby, or a sibling of a parent of the baby
- a child who is not your or your partner's child, who you became responsible for when they were aged one or older
- a child with whom you left your home due to domestic abuse

- a child who was born before you arrived in the UK, and you have been granted refugee status, humanitarian protection or leave in the UK under schemes for Ukrainian or Afghan nationals

The money is usually paid into your bank account. You do not need to repay it. You can spend the money on whatever you and your baby need most, and you do not have to provide evidence of what you have spent it on.

You may qualify for a Best Start grant pregnancy and baby payment if you are pregnant or have given birth in the last six months and you or your partner are entitled to certain qualifying benefits:

- universal credit
- income-related employment and support allowance
- pension credit
- housing benefit

You can also qualify for a Best Start grant pregnancy and baby payment without getting a qualifying benefit if you are aged under 18 when you apply, or aged under 20 and you are a dependant in someone else's benefit claim – eg, your parent is claiming child benefit for you while you are still at school or college studying Highers. You can apply in your own name, regardless of your age.

If you have a multiple birth, you get one multiple birth supplement of £383.75.

EXAMPLES

Multiple births

Maisie gives birth to twins. She has no other children. She is entitled to a grant of £767.50 for the first twin and £383.75 for the second twin, plus a £383.75 multiple birth supplement.

Eilidh has one child, aged three, and then has triplets. She is entitled to a grant of £383.75 for each triplet, plus a £383.75 multiple birth supplement.

You can apply for a Best Start grant pregnancy and baby payment from when you are 24 weeks pregnant, and up to six months after the birth. If your child is born alive at any stage of pregnancy and dies or is stillborn after 24 weeks of pregnancy, a grant is still payable, and does not have to be repaid. Chapter 8 has more information on financial help that is available if your child dies.

If you or your partner are waiting to hear about whether you are entitled to a qualifying benefit, do not delay claiming a Best Start grant. A decision may be put on hold or, if your claim is turned down, the decision can be changed if a qualifying benefit is awarded.

You use the same form to apply for Best Start foods and Best Start grant. Remember, you can qualify for Best Start foods from the start of pregnancy, and the pregnancy and baby payment from 24 weeks. If you are refused a Best Start grant because you have claimed too early, you can claim again when you are 24 weeks pregnant.

Help with NHS costs

You can get free NHS dental treatment and free prescriptions while you are pregnant and within one year of the birth of your baby. All medication and treatment is provided free of charge if you are a hospital inpatient, including around the birth, or while you are an outpatient or at a walk-in centre.

Depending on your income, you may be able to get help with other NHS costs, such as sight tests and glasses, wigs and fabric supports, and fares to hospital for you or your child. You do not have to pay for the cost of these if you or your partner receive certain qualifying benefits or are in an exempt group – eg, if you are a care leaver or an asylum seeker. The qualifying benefits are universal credit (provided your monthly earnings are under £435, or £935 if you have children or a health condition), income-related employment and support allowance (if you still get it) or the guarantee credit of pension credit. If you do not get a qualifying benefit but are on a low income, you may be able to get the item at a reduced cost.

In Scotland and Wales, everyone can get free prescriptions, wigs and fabric supports. Sight tests and NHS dental check-ups are also free in Scotland.

Are you working?

What the law says

Maternity rights at work

- It is against the law for your employer to sack you or force you to give up your job because you are pregnant.
- You have the right to reasonable paid time off for antenatal appointments.
- Your employer has a duty to carry out a health and safety assessment of any risks to you or your unborn baby associated with your job, such as heavy lifting or carrying, standing or sitting for long periods without adequate breaks, long working hours or exposure to toxic substances. You must notify your employer of your pregnancy in writing.
- If there are risks, your employer must take reasonable steps to remove them – eg, by offering you different work or changing your hours. If your employer cannot remove a risk, you should be suspended on full pay.
- As an employee, you have the right to 52 weeks' maternity leave.
- You have the right to statutory maternity pay if you meet the employment and earnings conditions. You can qualify if you are an employee, or an agency or casual worker.
- You have the right to return to your job after your maternity leave. If you take more than 26 weeks' maternity leave and it is not possible to return to the same job, your employer can give you a suitable alternative job.

See gov.uk/working-when-pregnant-your-rights.

If you are an employee (or an agency worker with at least 12 weeks in the same placement), it is up to you when to let your employer know you are pregnant. If you are taking maternity leave, you must tell your employer you are pregnant at least 15 weeks before your due date, or as soon as you can afterwards. You may need to tell your employer earlier so that you are protected by law and, depending on the type of work you do, you may want to ask for your duties to be adjusted.

Statutory maternity pay

If you work for an employer, you may be entitled to statutory maternity pay. This is paid to you as wages by your employer in the later stages of your pregnancy and after the birth, for a total of 39 weeks. Statutory maternity pay is the minimum the law requires employers to pay. You may be entitled to more generous contractual maternity pay, depending on the terms of your employment contract. You do not have to intend to go back to work in order to qualify for statutory maternity pay, and you do not have to repay it if you do not return to work.

If you meet the conditions, you have a legal right to statutory maternity pay and your employer is breaking the law if they refuse to pay it. If your employer dismisses you at any time while you are pregnant or after you have given birth, solely or mainly to avoid paying you statutory maternity pay, they are still liable to pay it. Employers can recover some or all of the statutory maternity pay they pay from the government. You may also be able to claim unfair dismissal. If you give up your job, you are dismissed or the job ends after your period of statutory maternity pay has begun, your employer is still liable to pay you until the end of the period.

If your baby is stillborn after the 24th week of pregnancy, or dies, statutory maternity pay is payable for the whole maternity pay period. Chapter 8 has more information on financial help that is available if your child dies.

Statutory maternity pay can be paid for a period of 39 consecutive weeks starting, at the earliest, from the 11th week before your baby is due and, at the latest, the day after the birth. If your baby is born earlier than the 11th week before the expected week, your statutory maternity pay begins on the day after the birth.

If your employer says that you are not entitled to statutory maternity pay and you disagree, you can contact the HM Revenue and Customs Statutory Payment Dispute Team on 0300 322 9422 (textphone: 0300 200 3212) to request a new decision.

If statutory maternity pay from your employer is your only or main income, you will usually be entitled to a top-up of universal credit. Statutory payments from your employer count as earned income for universal credit, which means a considerable amount is ignored.

Maternity allowance

If you have a recent work history but do not qualify for statutory maternity pay, you may be entitled to maternity allowance. This may be payable if you are self-employed, or if you have not worked for the same employer for long enough, or if your earnings are too low to get statutory maternity pay, or if you have recently stopped working. It is not means tested (ie, your income and savings are not taken into account) and it does not depend on your having paid national insurance contributions.

Maternity allowance is payable for a period of 39 consecutive weeks starting, at the earliest, from the 11th week before your baby is due and, at the latest, the day after the birth. If your baby is born earlier than the 11th week before they are due, maternity allowance begins on the day after the birth.

You can claim on form MA1 at any time after the end of the 15th week before your baby is due. You should also provide a maternity certificate (MAT B1), given to you by your GP or midwife, proof of having worked and evidence of your earnings. You may need to delay claiming if you will not meet the conditions until later in your pregnancy.

Maternity allowance can be backdated for up to three months. If your employer has told you that you are not entitled to statutory maternity pay and you claim maternity allowance within three months of this notification, your claim can be backdated to the date you notified your employer that you wanted to apply for statutory maternity pay.

If maternity allowance is your only or main income, you can usually get a top-up of universal credit to help with living costs for you and your baby, and for help with rent. Maternity allowance counts in full as unearned income for universal credit. In some cases, especially if you are single and not liable for rent, the amount of maternity allowance may be too high for you to get universal credit, even after your child is born, which means you cannot qualify for additional support such as Sure Start, Healthy Start or Best Start payments. You have the option to give up maternity allowance and claim universal credit instead. Maternity allowance cannot be counted against you if you have stopped receiving it or decided not to claim it. If you are in this situation, get advice about when you may be better off doing this.

Employment and support allowance

You may be entitled to employment and support allowance if you are unable to work during your pregnancy and around the birth, or at other times due to illness, depending on your national insurance record. It is not affected by savings or a partner's income. You may qualify for employment and support allowance if you have a sufficient national insurance record and:

- you are entitled to maternity allowance during pregnancy. If you are only entitled to a reduced rate of maternity allowance, it can be topped up by employment and support allowance
- for the period of six weeks before the due date and two weeks after the birth you are not entitled to maternity allowance or statutory maternity pay
- you are pregnant and work would pose a serious risk to your or your baby's health

At other times you may qualify if you provide medical evidence of limited capability for work – eg, if you have a pregnancy-related illness, post-natal depression or other health condition or disability.

Box D

Are you still getting income-related employment and support allowance?

If you have a long-term health condition or disability and are still getting income-related employment and support allowance, you can continue to get this during pregnancy and it is a qualifying benefit for other financial help. When your baby is born, you will need to claim universal credit instead to get support for yourself and your baby. You can make a claim for this before the birth.

At the time of writing, the government was in the process of stopping income-related employment and support allowance (by the end of March 2026), sending claimants a migration notice (by September 2025) telling them to make a claim for universal credit instead.

3. How are your benefits affected if you are pregnant?

Do you have to look for work?

If you have to look for work in order to get benefit, tell your work coach at the job centre that you are pregnant as soon as you can. You can agree restrictions on the hours or type of work you are looking for. You are usually still expected to look for work until 11 weeks before the week your baby is due, unless you have a pregnancy-related illness or there is a risk to you or your baby. You can agree that there are certain types of work that would not be suitable for you – eg, jobs that involve prolonged standing or heavy physical tasks.

If you are claiming jobseeker's allowance while you are pregnant, you must continue to be available for work and looking for work, within limits as agreed. If you are sick during your pregnancy, you may be able to continue on jobseeker's allowance for up to 13 weeks, if you provide medical evidence of your illness.

When you have 11 weeks to go before your baby is due, you usually have the option to stop claiming jobseeker's allowance, so that you no longer have to look for work. This means you can usually make a new claim for universal credit.

If you are claiming universal credit while you are pregnant, your work-related requirements might not change for the first 29 weeks, so you may still have to be available for work and look for work, within limits as agreed. You cannot have any work-related requirements imposed on you from 11 weeks before your baby is due until 15 weeks after the birth, or while you are the main carer of a child under the age of one.

EXAMPLE

Switching from jobseeker's allowance to universal credit

Selena is six months pregnant and is getting jobseeker's allowance. She has already asked for her claimant commitment to be adjusted so that she does not have to look for work that involves standing for long periods, and this has been agreed. However, she is finding looking for work and applying for jobs stressful. When there are 11 weeks to go before her due date, she can claim universal credit and does not have any work-related requirements. When her baby is born, she should report the birth so that she gets a child element for her baby.

If you are claiming universal credit as a couple, your partner must usually still meet all their work-related requirements right up to, and after, the birth. However, they should notify their work coach of when your baby is due and get this recorded in their claimant commitment. If they fail to meet their work-related requirements as agreed because they have to be with you suddenly due to your pregnancy or going into labour, they should explain this as soon as possible to avoid a sanction being imposed and their benefit reduced.

Chapter 5 has more information about your work-related requirements.

Are you at risk of being sanctioned?

If you do not do what you have agreed to do to look for work, there is a risk that you will be sanctioned. A sanction means your benefit is reduced. You can challenge a decision to impose a sanction. A sanction should not be imposed if you have a good reason for not doing what was expected of you. A good reason may be related to your pregnancy – eg, if you missed an appointment because you had to get urgent medical attention. For universal credit, when there are 11 weeks or less before your baby is due, and for 15 weeks after the birth, or while you are responsible for a baby under one, you have no work-related requirements and cannot be sanctioned.

If you are sanctioned while pregnant and claiming universal credit or jobseeker's allowance, you can request hardship payments of your universal credit or jobseeker's allowance. You must show that you are in hardship. You can apply straight away for these because you are considered to be vulnerable due to pregnancy. You must still meet your work-related requirements or jobseeking conditions as agreed.

If you are claiming universal credit, you must reapply for hardship payments at the end of each monthly universal credit assessment period. Hardship payments of universal credit are recoverable, so you must accept that you will have to pay them back once the sanction has ended.

When there are 11 weeks or less before your baby is due, the amount of the sanction in universal credit should be adjusted automatically, so that you are left with an amount of benefit that is equivalent to the amount of a hardship payment. The sanction should not be increased within 15 weeks of the birth, and while you are responsible for a child under the age of one.

Chapter 11 has more information on what you should do if you have been sanctioned, or threatened with a sanction.

Do you have a disability or are you ill?

If you have a disability or long-term health condition, or you become ill during your pregnancy, this may make a difference to your benefit entitlement and what you are expected to do in return for benefit.

Pregnancy, in itself, is not considered an illness, but you may be considered to have a pregnancy-related illness (eg, severe morning sickness) if this is confirmed by medical evidence. Your entitlement may also change if there are complications with your pregnancy which put you or your baby at risk.

If you are claiming universal credit or jobseeker's allowance and are not well enough to look for work, tell your work coach at the job centre. You may be asked to provide medical evidence from your doctor. You are allowed two periods of sickness of up to two weeks in any 12-month period, during which time you are not required to look for work. For universal credit, the DWP has the discretion to extend this period, or allow more than two periods of illness. For jobseeker's allowance, you are also allowed one extended period of sickness of up to 13 weeks. You still need to be willing and able to take up work when you are feeling better.

If you are not well enough to look for work at all during your pregnancy, you may be able to claim employment and support allowance (depending on your national insurance contributions) without being required to look for work. You may still be required to attend work-focused interviews or prepare for work. You can qualify for employment and support allowance while you are pregnant if you are entitled to maternity allowance, or if you are within six weeks of the date your baby is due or 14 days after giving birth.

If your doctor says there is a serious risk to your health or to your baby's health if you work or prepare for work, you can claim employment and support allowance or universal credit without being required to look for work or prepare for work.

Chapter 7 has more information on benefits for people with a disability or long-term health condition.

4. What help can you get when your baby is born?

Are you working or on maternity leave?

If you were working right up to the day your baby was born, **statutory maternity leave**, and **statutory maternity pay** if you are entitled to it, must start the day after the birth at the latest. Statutory maternity leave is 52 weeks. You do not have to take the full 52 weeks, but must take at least two weeks after your baby is born, or four weeks if you work in a factory.

Your baby's father, or your partner, may also qualify for **statutory paternity leave and pay** to be able to take two weeks off work to support you and care for the baby.

If you and the baby's father, or your partner, want to share the care of your baby in the first year, you may qualify for **statutory shared parental leave and pay**. You must take at least two weeks' statutory maternity leave (four weeks if you work in a factory) – you can then decide to give it up for statutory shared parental leave and pay instead. This allows you to divide the leave more flexibly (eg, taking three months each) or take time off at the same time.

If your baby needs hospital treatment for at least seven days starting within 28 days of the day after the birth, you and the baby's father, or your partner, may be entitled to up to 12 weeks' **statutory neonatal care leave and pay**, which can be taken after maternity leave has ended. Fathers or partners can take neonatal care leave and pay when the baby is in hospital or immediately after paternity leave if they are on leave at the time.

If statutory maternity pay or other statutory payments from your employer are your only or main income, you will usually be entitled to a top-up of universal credit. Statutory payments from your employer count as earned income for universal credit, which means a considerable amount is ignored.

Child benefit

You should claim child benefit as soon as you can after your baby is born and you have registered the birth.

You can claim online at gov.uk or you can find the claim form in the bounty pack usually given to new mothers in hospital.

Almost everyone with children can get child benefit, although you may not be entitled if your immigration status does not allow you to claim benefits, or if your baby is taken into care. You must be living with your baby or contributing at least the amount of child benefit to support them.

You can claim child benefit if you are under 16. Alternatively, if you live with your parent(s) or guardian, they can claim child benefit for both you and your baby instead. However, you get £8.80 a week more if you claim yourself, because a higher amount is payable for a person's first child.

If you are already getting child benefit for another child, you must still complete the claim form and fill in the relevant section about other children.

You only need to provide a reference number from the birth certificate if the birth has been registered in Great Britain. If the birth was not registered in Great Britain, you must usually send your baby's original birth certificate with the claim form, and it will be returned to you within four weeks.

Child benefit can only be backdated for three months, so it is important not to delay making a new claim for more than three months, or you will lose money. It can take up to 16 weeks for child benefit claims to be processed.

What CPAG says

Everyone entitled to child benefit should claim it

Child benefit is payable to all families, regardless of their income. However, if you have a high income, you may have to pay some, or all, of it back through income tax.

For every £200 of your taxable income over £60,000, you must pay 1 per cent of your child benefit back. If your income is over £80,000, you must pay the full amount of child benefit back as income tax. This rule applies to your or your partner's individual income, not to your joint income.

You should still claim child benefit as it protects your national insurance record by giving you entitlement to national insurance credits that count towards your state pension. Claiming child benefit for your child also means that they will automatically be issued a national insurance number when they turn 16.

It is also helpful to have made a claim, so that you can receive child benefit as soon as possible if your income goes down, or if you separate from your partner or you are bereaved.

You can claim child benefit and choose not to receive it if you would rather not go through the process of completing a tax return and paying it back through income tax.

Universal credit

If you get universal credit, you can get an extra amount for your baby. You can make a new claim during maternity or other leave. The amount you get depends on maternity pay or other income. You may be entitled once your baby is born, even if your income was too high to qualify during pregnancy.

If you are already getting universal credit, you should report on your online journal that you have had your baby. You are entitled to an additional amount (a child element), worth £292.81 a month. Make sure you tell your work coach or notify the change online, by phone or in writing before the end of the assessment period in which your baby is born. You are entitled to the child element for all of that month. If you leave it late, you may miss out unless there were special circumstances that meant you could not notify the birth earlier. You have no work-related requirements while your child is under age one. When your child is one, you can be required to attend work-focused interviews. When your child is two, you can be required to undertake activities to prepare for work. When your child is three, you can be required to look for, and be available for, work, within limits and depending on suitable available childcare.

Note: if you are already responsible for two or more children, you may not get extra universal credit for a new baby (see Box E).

Box E

Have you got two or more children?

If you already have two or more children, you cannot usually get a child element for a new baby. This is called the two-child limit. There are exceptions to this rule, as listed below.

- You have a multiple birth (eg, twins or triplets) and have no other children or just one other child. In this case, you can get a child element for all the children in the multiple birth. If you already have two or more children, you can get a child element for all but one of the children in the multiple birth.
- You have adopted a child from local authority care.
- You are under 16 and someone else is claiming universal credit for you – their benefit includes an amount for your baby.
- You are not the child's parent, but you have taken responsibility for them under specific legal provisions, or you receive guardian's allowance for them, or a social worker confirms that the child would otherwise be at risk of being taken into care.
- Your child is likely to have been conceived as a result of rape or a coercive or controlling relationship, and you are not living with the perpetrator.

What families say

The two-child limit

'With the unexpected pregnancy with my 3rd, I've found myself in this desperate situation... I just couldn't believe that as a single parent I won't get any extra support for my 3rd child. I was shocked and then in panic, thinking, how will I cope? ... As a lone parent I don't have any financial backup from a partner. It's shocking that I don't get more support for my 3rd baby in this situation.' *Single mum, Early Warning System*

You should always report the birth of a new baby to the DWP, as this can affect your work-related requirements and other support may be available. If an older child leaves the household so that there is only one other child included in your claim, you can start to receive a child element for your younger child.

If your child has a disability and gets disability living allowance or child disability payment, a disabled child addition is payable, even if the basic child amount is not payable for them because of the two-child limit.

What CPAG says

The two-child limit

CPAG believes that limiting universal credit to two children is morally wrong. It contravenes the rights of the child and the right to family life, as well as breaching human rights in other specific cases – eg, because of religious or conscientious beliefs about contraception or abortion. Legal challenges have so far been unsuccessful, but CPAG will continue to campaign for the abolition of the two-child limit. At the time of writing, the UK government is under increasing pressure to scrap the two-child limit, and the Scottish government is planning to introduce a new payment from March 2026 for people affected by it.

If you are paying for childcare, you should report your total childcare costs for all your children, as these can be included in universal credit, even if the basic child element is not payable because of the two-child limit. Chapter 4 has more information on getting help with paying for childcare.

Remember that the two-child limit only applies to universal credit. There is no two-child limit for child benefit, pension credit, Healthy Start, Best Start grants and foods or Scottish child payment.

Healthy Start scheme and vitamins

Remember to notify Healthy Start once your baby is born in order to continue getting payments and vitamins. You get an extra amount during your baby's first year.

If you did not qualify during pregnancy, you may now qualify, especially if you are now entitled to universal credit. If your child is a British citizen and you would qualify through universal credit but you are excluded from benefits because of your immigration status, your child can qualify for Healthy Start.

Sure Start maternity grant

If you did not qualify for a Sure Start maternity grant while you were pregnant, check whether you qualify now, especially if you are getting universal credit.

You must apply for a Sure Start maternity grant within six months of your baby's birth. Even if you have claimed and are waiting to hear about universal credit, you should still apply for a Sure Start maternity grant within six months of the birth.

Best Start in Scotland

Contact Social Security Scotland when your baby is born. If you are already getting Best Start foods, the amount is increased for a baby under one. If your income is below a certain level but you are excluded from benefits due to your immigration status, your child can get Best Start foods. If you did not qualify for Best Start foods or a Best Start grant during pregnancy, you may qualify if you are now entitled to universal credit. You must usually claim the Best Start grant pregnancy and baby payment within six months of the birth.

When your child is aged two, you may be entitled to the Best Start grant early learning payment. This is £319.80 per child aged two to three and six months. You can apply at any time from their second birthday until six months after their third birthday, as long as you meet the qualifying conditions when you apply.

When your child is able to start school, you can apply for the Best Start grant school age payment. This is £319.80 per child, payable from 1 June in the calendar year that they turn five or, if they were born in January or February, the calendar year in which they turn four – you must claim before the end of February in the following year. This ties in with when your child is able to start school, but it does not matter whether they have actually started school or not – eg, if you have deferred their place.

You need not have received the pregnancy and baby payment in order to receive the early learning payment or school age payment.

If you are getting Scottish child payment for your child, the early learning and school age payments may be paid automatically.

Scottish child payment

Scottish child payment is an additional payment for families living in Scotland to top up means-tested benefits by an extra £27.15 a week for each child under 16. You qualify if you are responsible for a child under 16, and you or your partner are getting any amount of:

- universal credit
- income-related employment and support allowance
- pension credit

You can still get Scottish child payment if universal credit has been reduced to nil due to a sanction. You can still get the payment even if you are not getting an extra element for the child in universal credit due to the two-child limit. You can get Scottish child payment if you are a kinship carer and you are getting one of these benefits for yourself and the child lives with you.

You can get child benefit and universal credit child elements as well as Scottish child payment.

What families say

Confusing Scottish child payment with child benefit

'When a new mum contacted Social Security Scotland about claiming Scottish child payment and Best Start grant, she said she was told she could get Scottish child payment or child benefit, but not both. She claimed Scottish child payment and did not find out she could also get child benefit until a year later. As child benefit can only be backdated for up to three months, the family lost out on nine months of child benefit.'
Early Warning System

5. Are you a young parent?

If you are a young parent, you may have a choice about whether you are entitled to some support in your own right or whether someone else (usually your parent or guardian) claims for you.

What CPAG says

Advice for young parents

- You do not have to give up your education or training.
- You do not have to give up work.
- If you live with your parents, get advice on whether they should claim benefits for you, or whether you should make a claim yourself – the amount may be different.
- If you live on your own, you can claim benefits as a lone parent.
- If your partner lives with you (they do not have to be your baby's parent) and you are both aged at least 16, you count as a couple and their income may affect your benefits.

If you are under 16, you can claim child benefit for your child in your own right. You could also be entitled to maternity allowance if you have been working – even a weekend or part-time job could be enough to qualify.

You cannot claim universal credit until you reach the age of 16. If you are 16 or 17 and pregnant, you cannot usually get universal credit until 11 weeks before your due date, but you can qualify earlier if you are without parental support. If you are still in non-advanced education or training, you cannot usually get universal credit during pregnancy, unless you are under 21 and without parental support. Being without parental support means you are orphaned or estranged, or at risk of harm if you lived with your parents, and have no one else acting in the place of your parents.

When your baby is born and you are responsible for them, you can claim universal credit if you are 16 or over, whether or not you are in education or without parental support. You do not have to look for work or have any other work-related requirements in order to receive universal credit from 11 weeks before your due date and while your baby is under one.

If you are aged 16 to 19 and still in non-advanced education or training, you may be able to choose between claiming universal credit for yourself and your baby, or allowing someone else to claim or to continue claiming universal credit for you and your baby as their dependent children. In this situation, there are a lot of things to consider, such as whether you want the financial independence of being responsible for your own money, and whether you would be better off – the amounts can work out very differently depending on your circumstances.

If someone else is claiming universal credit for you and your baby, they can also claim a Sure Start maternity grant or Best Start grant for your baby.

You are entitled to a Healthy Start payment card and vitamins (or Best Start foods in Scotland) while you are pregnant and under 18. For Best Start foods, you are also entitled if you are under 20 and someone else is claiming a qualifying benefit for you.

6. Are you adopting a child?

If you are adopting a child, financial help is available, some of which depends on the age of the child.

This section applies to you if you have formally adopted a child and an adoption order has been granted in your favour by the court, and when a child has been placed with you before formal adoption has taken place.

- You can qualify for a Sure Start maternity grant (in England and Wales) if you are adopting a child under 12 months, and you are getting a qualifying benefit. You must claim within six months of the date the child is placed with you for adoption, and before the child's first birthday. You cannot usually qualify if there is another child aged under 16 in your family, but you can if that child was over 12 months old when you became responsible for them.
- You can qualify for a Best Start grant pregnancy and baby payment (in Scotland) if a child under 12 months has been placed with you by an adoption agency, and you are getting a qualifying benefit. You must apply before the child's first birthday.
- You may be entitled to statutory adoption pay instead of statutory maternity pay. Statutory adoption pay is payable for 39 weeks, starting from (at the earliest) 14 days before the date you expect the child to be placed with you. If you are jointly adopting a child with your partner, either of you may be entitled to statutory adoption pay, but only one of you can claim it. If you get statutory adoption pay, your partner may be entitled to statutory paternity pay. You can decide to give up your statutory adoption pay and take statutory shared parental pay between you instead.
- You are entitled to child benefit under the normal rules.
- You can get a child element in your universal credit or pension credit. This includes if the child is placed with you while they are still being looked after by the local authority. The two-child limit does not apply, so you still get an amount for an adopted child even if you have two or more other children. Report the change as soon as the child is normally living with you.

- Adoption allowances that you use to spend on the child do not affect your entitlement to benefits.
- You can get a Healthy Start payment card and vitamins for a child aged under four who is placed with you for adoption if you get universal credit for them. In Scotland, you can get Best Start foods if a child has been placed with you by an adoption agency and you get a qualifying benefit.

7. Are you taking on responsibility for a child in other circumstances?

If you are taking on responsibility for a child in other circumstances, you may be entitled to some of the financial help mentioned in this chapter. This might apply to you if the child is normally living with you and:

- you or your partner are not the child's mother
- you have been granted a parental order following a surrogate pregnancy
- you are the guardian of the child (eg, if their parents have died) – you can also get a benefit called guardian's allowance in this case
- you have been granted a child arrangements order or kinship care order

In these cases, you can qualify for a Sure Start maternity grant or Best Start grant if the child is under 12 months old, and you are getting a qualifying benefit. The grant is payable even if one has already been paid to someone else. You can also qualify for Healthy Start or Best Start foods in these circumstances, if you are getting a qualifying benefit.

You can usually get child benefit in these circumstances. If one or both of the child's parents has died, you may also be able to get guardian's allowance. You may be able to get a child element in universal credit or pension credit, but a child element is not usually payable while the child is in the care of the local authority, unless you have parental responsibility. You may be able to get other financial help from your local authority. There is more information in Chapter 9 about when a child is in care.

You cannot get statutory maternity or adoption leave or pay in these circumstances, but you may have a right to unpaid parental leave if you have, or expect to have, parental responsibility for the child.

Are you over pension age?

If you (and your partner if you are part of a couple) are over pension age, you may be entitled to pension credit, depending on your income. You cannot usually get universal credit. If you have responsibility for a child, pension credit includes additional amounts for children. Pension credit is not affected by the two-child limit or the benefit cap. Pension credit has no work-related requirements and cannot be sanctioned. It does not include any help with childcare costs.

You may be entitled to pension-age housing benefit to help with your rent, and this is not affected by the bedroom tax.

You may qualify for a Sure Start maternity grant or a Best Start grant pregnancy and baby payment if you have taken on reponsibility for a baby under one.

You may also qualify for Healthy Start or Best Start foods.

You can get child benefit.

If you get pension credit, live in Scotland and are responsible for a child under 16, you can get Scottish child payment.

If you are part of a couple and one of you is over pension age and the other is under pension age, you cannot usually claim pension credit, and must still claim universal credit until you are both over pension age.

Further information

Maternity Action provides free advice on rights at work, maternity pay and benefits to pregnant women, new mothers and fathers, trade unions, advisers and employers: maternityaction.org.uk
Maternity rights advice line: 0808 802 0029

Working Families gives advice on employment rights for parents and on benefits for families: workingfamilies.org.uk
Helpline: 0300 012 0312

Family Lives offers information, advice, guidance and support on any aspect of parenting and family life: familylives.org.uk
Helpline: 0808 800 2222

One Parent Families Scotland provides support and advice on anything from dealing with a break-up, to moving into work and sorting out maintenance or benefit issues: opfs.org.uk
Helpline: 0808 801 0323

Chapter 3
Child maintenance

This chapter covers:

1. What help is available?
2. How do you apply for child maintenance?
3. How much money do you get?
4. What should you do if your circumstances change?
5. Are you unhappy with the amount of maintenance you get?
6. Do you pay child maintenance to someone?

What you need to know

- If you are the main carer of a child and their other parent lives elsewhere, you can get financial help from that person.
- You can choose to arrange this by yourself or use a government scheme. Some parents can use the courts.
- Child maintenance does not affect your benefits, so it can really help with the costs of bringing up children.

1. What help is available?

All parents are legally obliged to support their children financially until they are 16, and sometimes until they are 20. If you are the main carer for your child and their other parent does not live with you, you may be able to get child maintenance – money the other parent pays you to help with the costs of your child. Child maintenance is often called child support.

You can also get child maintenance if you are the main carer for someone else's child and their parents live elsewhere. For example, if you are a grandparent who is the main carer of a child, you may be able to get child maintenance from both parents.

You do not have to arrange or apply for child maintenance if you do not want to. It does not affect any of your benefits. As long as it is money for your children, it is paid on top of all benefits to which you are entitled. You may also get maintenance for yourself. If this is the case, this *does* count as income and could affect your benefits.

2. How do you apply for child maintenance?

When can you get child maintenance?

If you have children who live, or mainly live, with you, and one or both of their parents live elsewhere, you may be able to get child maintenance from the parents. If your children have different parents, you can get maintenance from all of them.

The children must be under 16, or under 20 and a qualifying young person for the purposes of child benefit. The main condition for being a qualifying young person is that the young person is still in full-time, non-advanced education. This means education at a school or college, studying for GCSEs, A levels, Scottish Highers and other courses that are below university level.

A child for whom you can get child maintenance is known as a qualifying child.

EXAMPLE

Getting maintenance

Rihanna has three children living with her. Louie is 18 and doing an apprenticeship. Alex and Patrice are six. Rihanna can get child maintenance for the twins, but not for Louie as he is not a qualifying child. The apprenticeship does not count as non-advanced education.

Do you want to apply?

You must decide whether you want to get child maintenance. There are lots of factors to consider, including whether the other parent sees the children and how much time they spend together.

If you are worried about how child maintenance might affect a child's relationship with their other parent, it may help to discuss this. You can talk to an organisation that supports separated parents.

What are your options?

If you decide you want child maintenance, the next step is to decide which option to choose.

- You can agree something with your child's other parent: a family-based arrangement.
- You can apply to the Child Maintenance Service, which is a government agency. It runs a child maintenance scheme based on regulations (legal rules).
- You can make an agreement with the other parent that becomes legally binding through the courts. People who have been married to each other often use this option.

What is a family-based arrangement?

A family-based arrangement means that you and the other parent decide how much maintenance will be paid and when. If the other parent stops paying, you cannot take any enforcement action. Mediation can help you to decide on the terms of the arrangement and can be cheaper than legal advice.

You can use the 'get help arranging child maintenance' tool on the gov.uk website to help you understand child maintenance and which option would suit you best. The tool has a child maintenance calculator you can use to check how much the other parent would pay if you made an application to the Child Maintenance Service. Alternatively, you can work out an amount that reflects the costs of your children and how you want to share these costs. The tool has a form you can use to write down the details of your agreement with the other parent. However, it is important to understand that writing it down does not make it legally binding.

EXAMPLE

A family-based arrangement

Rae and Ian are separated. Their child Charlotte lives most of the time with Rae, but Ian helps to collect Charlotte from school and also looks after her during the school holidays.

Rae and Ian come to an agreement based on the 'get help arranging child maintenance' calculator and negotiate so the amount reflects their different costs and income. Ian pays £70 a week in term time, but less in school holidays. This works well for Rae, but if Ian stopped paying or reduced the amount, she would not be able to make him pay the agreed amount.

What is the Child Maintenance Service?

The Child Maintenance Service calculates child maintenance (child support) for people who apply and who are eligible. You can apply to the Child Maintenance Service for it to work out how much child maintenance the other parent should pay, using rules (regulations) set by government.

The Child Maintenance Service usually prefers the other parent to pay the child maintenance to you directly. This is known as direct pay. If you have experienced domestic abuse, you should tell the Child Maintenance Service and it should explain how to make a direct pay agreement that will keep you safe. Alternatively, it can collect the money from the other parent and then pay you. This is known as collect and pay. You cannot choose this option unless the other parent agrees or there is a problem with payment. If the other parent does not pay you or fails to pay the correct amount, tell the Child Maintenance Service and ask it to use collect and pay. However, using collect and pay means that the paying parent pays an extra 20 per cent and the money you receive is reduced by 4 per cent.

Before using the Child Maintenance Service, you must use the 'get help arranging child maintenance' tool, which explains child maintenance on behalf of the government. You cannot make an application without going through this first. The tool describes the advantages and disadvantages of family-based arrangements and more formal arrangements like the Child Maintenance Service or the courts, and explains the costs of using the Child Maintenance Service if these apply.

Box A

Pros and cons of child maintenance arrangements

Family-based	Child Maintenance Service
Can agree a higher amount.	Amount is set by the government's calculation, and there is a maximum amount even if the other parent is a very high earner.
Can adjust by agreement.	Changes in circumstances must be reported to the Child Maintenance Service, and only changes which affect the calculation are taken into account.
No fees.	No application fee, but there is a deduction from collect and pay.
Can arrange payment to suit.	Payment amounts are fixed. Collect and pay is not always possible, reduces the amount of your maintenance and costs the other parent.
Could avoid conflict.	Could create, or worsen, conflict with the other parent and could lead to disagreement about any shared care.
Not possible if you cannot negotiate.	Does not require communication with the other parent.
Cannot be enforced.	Can be enforced according to set rules – but only if the Child Maintenance Service decides to take action.

EXAMPLE

Child Maintenance Service collect and pay fees

Yolande's four children live with her. The Child Maintenance Service calculates that her former partner Ben, who is the father of all four children, should pay Yolande £35 a week child maintenance. If direct pay is used, Ben pays £35 a week directly to Yolande.

If the collect and pay service is used, Ben pays £42 a week (£35 + (20 per cent x £35)) to the Child Maintenance Service. It deducts £1.40 (4 per cent x £35) from the child maintenance due to Yolande, so she receives only £33.60 a week. The Child Maintenance Service keeps the balance of £8.40 a week.

What about going to court?

A child maintenance agreement can be made into a formally binding agreement through the courts system. This is called a consent order in England and Wales, and a registered minute of agreement in Scotland. Mediation may help you to decide on the terms of the agreement, to avoid higher legal costs – but in Scotland, the agreement is usually written by your solicitor.

A binding agreement like this means that, if the other parent stops paying maintenance, you can go back to court to get the order enforced (made to happen). However, after the order has been in force for at least a year, you (or the other parent) could also choose to make an application to the Child Maintenance Service. This means that, after the first year, it is harder to have this kind of agreement enforced.

Usually, the courts are used when parents are divorcing and the order includes other issues – eg, payment of a mortgage. However, it is not necessary to use the courts and it can be a lot cheaper not to do so, if parents can agree.

Box B

Pros and cons of going to court

Advantages	Disadvantages
Can include other issues, such as housing costs.	May require legal advice, which usually has to be paid for.
Can be enforced through the court.	Involves fees and a formal court process.
	Changing the payments means applying to the court.
	Getting the order enforced can cost money and may be harder to do after the first year.
	Once you have a consent order or a registered minute of agreement, you cannot apply to the Child Maintenance Service for the next 12 months. After that, the other parent can apply to the Child Maintenance Service, which may be likely if the amount they would pay under the calculation is lower than that under the court order. This application then overrides the consent order or registered minute of agreement.

3. How much money do you get?

If you make an agreement with the other parent, the amount of child maintenance you get depends on what you agree. You can do this as part of a mediation process, or you may be able to have the conversation without using a mediator. You can use the calculator provided by the 'get help arranging child maintenance' tool as a guide.

If you apply to the Child Maintenance Service, the amount of child maintenance is based on the circumstances of the other parent and the number of children.

The other parent's gross weekly income is used in the calculation. This is income before tax and national insurance are deducted. It includes their earnings, pension income and some other taxable income. If you think they have other income, you can ask for an additional/unearned income variation. This means other income such as interest on savings, rent from property or dividends can be included.

Only the other parent's income is taken into account. If they live with a new partner, the partner's income is ignored.

There are different rates of maintenance.

Some parents do not have to pay anything. This is called the nil rate. It applies to very young parents (those for whom someone still receives child benefit, or those who are under 18 and get universal credit with no earnings), prisoners, some people in care homes or independent hospitals, and some people who have a very low income.

If the other parent is on certain benefits or has an income of £100 a week or less, they pay a flat rate of £7 a week.

A reduced rate of maintenance applies if the other parent's gross income is over £100 but under £200 a week. In this case, the other parent pays £7 a week plus a percentage of the amount of income they have over £100 a week:

- 17 per cent for one child
- 25 per cent for two children
- 31 per cent for three or more children

These percentages are reduced if the other parent has other children living with them. The amount of the reduction depends on the number of children.

EXAMPLE

Reduced-rate child maintenance

Mia has two children. Their father Tim does not live with them and only occasionally sees the family.

Tim works variable hours at the minimum wage, but over the last few months his gross earnings have averaged £180 a week. Mia applies to the Child Maintenance Service and the reduced rate is used. Tim's weekly income is £80 above the £100 threshold. Twenty-five per cent of £80 = £20. This is added to £7. Tim must pay £27 a week.

Otherwise, a parent pays the basic rate of maintenance. This is worked out by first deducting an amount from the other parent's gross weekly income for any other children living with them:

- 11 per cent of gross income for one child
- 14 per cent of gross income for two children
- 16 per cent of gross income for three or more children

Once the deduction has been made, if the parent's remaining gross weekly income is £800 or less, they pay the following percentage of their income in maintenance:

- 12 per cent for one child
- 16 per cent for two children
- 19 per cent for three or more children

If the parent's remaining gross weekly income is over £800, they pay the relevant percentage above of the first £800 of their income in maintenance *plus* an additional percentage of any income over £800:

- 9 per cent for one child
- 12 per cent for two children
- 15 per cent for three or more children

If a parent is paying child maintenance for children who have different other parents, the child maintenance due is split between those other parents. It is split in proportion to the number of children each of the other parents is looking after.

EXAMPLES

Basic-rate child maintenance

Pretesh and Joni are separated and have two children, aged 12 and eight. Joni has the main care of the children. Pretesh comes to see them once a week, but does not stay overnight. Pretesh has one younger child who lives with him and his new partner. Pretesh earns £650 a week gross.

Joni applies to the Child Maintenance Service and the basic rate is used. Pretesh's income is first reduced by 11 per cent because he has one child living with him – giving £578.50. Pretesh then pays 16 per cent of £578.50 = £92.56 a week. The £92.56 is paid on top of any benefits Joni receives and can go directly to support the family.

Consuela and Fred are separated with one child. Fred visits, but does not stay overnight. Fred earns £1,200 a week gross and has no other children.

Consuela applies to the Child Maintenance Service and the basic rate is used. First, looking at Fred's income up to £800, 12 per cent of £800 = £96 basic maintenance. Next, Fred has £400 income above £800. Nine per cent of £400 = £36 additional maintenance. So the total amount of maintenance he must pay is £96 plus £36 = £132 a week.

EXAMPLE

Apportionment

Rhys has two children. Rosie lives with her mother Kate. Jack lives with his mother Kelly. Rhys is due to pay £39 a week child maintenance. As Kate and Kelly each look after one child, the child maintenance is split equally between them and they each receive £19.50 a week from Rhys.

If some children of a relationship live with one parent and the other children live with the other parent, both parents may have to pay child maintenance. The payments are usually offset, so that only the parent who owes more actually pays anything.

EXAMPLE

Divided families

Nick and Amanda are separated. They have two children, Kameron and Kirsten. Kameron lives with Nick and Kirsten lives with Amanda.

Both Nick and Amanda have to pay child maintenance for one child. Their gross weekly incomes are different. Nick is due to pay Amanda £54 a week for Kirsten. Amanda is due to pay Nick £24 a week for Kameron. The payments due are offset, so Nick pays Amanda £30 a week (£54 – £24).

Does the other parent also look after the child?

If the other parent looks after the child overnight for at least one night a week (on average), this reduces the amount of child maintenance they must pay under the Child Maintenance Service calculation.

A parent who pays the basic or reduced rate of maintenance has this amount reduced by:

- one-seventh for 52 to 103 nights of care a year
- two-sevenths for 104 to 155 nights of care a year
- three-sevenths for 156 to 174 nights of care a year
- one-half for 175 or more nights of care a year

If the day-to-day care of your child is shared absolutely equally between you and the other parent, there may be no child maintenance liability, even if the other parent earns more than you. You could still make a family-based arrangement.

EXAMPLE

Shared care

Tim moves into a new flat and is able to have the children stay with him for two nights a week on a regular basis, which Mia is happy with. The amount of child maintenance he must pay is reduced by two-sevenths of £27 = £7.71. He must now pay £19.29 a week.

4. What should you do if your circumstances change?

If your circumstances, or the other parent's circumstances, change, you may need to stop child maintenance or change the amount you get. For example, if a child no longer lives with you, your child maintenance could stop or the amount could go down. If the other parent gets a better paying job, the amount of your child maintenance could increase.

EXAMPLE

Change of circumstances

Amara's eldest son is 18 and leaves school in the summer. Because he is no longer in full-time, non-advanced education, his father Jon no longer needs to pay child maintenance for him. However, Jon's two other children are under 16 and still living with her. Amara has a family-based arrangement and agrees that the child maintenance she gets will reduce. Even though her son continues to live with her, she cannot force Jon to pay maintenance for him, even if she was using the Child Maintenance Service or the courts.

If you have a family-based arrangement, you should discuss the change with the other parent. You can still use the 'get help arranging child maintenance' service calculator as a guide.

If you are using the Child Maintenance Service, tell it about the change so that it can check the calculation.

If you have a court order, you will need to apply to the court to change the amount.

5. Are you unhappy with the amount of maintenance you get?

If you get child maintenance under a family-based arrangement, but are not happy with the amount, you could try to negotiate with the other parent. There might be specific expenses they could help with, such as school trips, or they may agree to pay more on a regular basis. Alternatively, you could consider using the Child Maintenance Service. Get advice to check whether the Child Maintenance Service calculation will result in your getting more money.

If you are using the Child Maintenance Service, but you think the calculation does not represent the other parent's actual income, you can ask for a variation. A variation allows the calculation to be altered to take into account a different level of income. Variations can only be made in certain situations – eg, if you think the other parent has income which has not been taken into account in the calculation or has substantial assets, you can apply for a variation.

What should you do if the other parent is not paying?

If the other parent is not paying, your options depend on the sort of child maintenance you have arranged.

If you have a family-based arrangement, you cannot force the other parent to pay. You may be able to negotiate. If you cannot find a way forward, you could consider making an application to the Child Maintenance Service.

If you are using the Child Maintenance Service, you can ask it to enforce payment. If you are using collect and pay, the Child Maintenance Service will know that payments have stopped. If the other parent pays you directly, tell the Child Maintenance Service that payment has stopped.

If you have a court order, you must apply to the court to enforce it.

6. Do you pay child maintenance to someone?

If you or your partner pay child maintenance to your child's other parent or main carer and you also have other children who live with you, or you provide some care for children who do not live with you full time, you should check that the amount you pay reflects these circumstances. You could use the Child Maintenance Service calculator to do this, even if there is no application to the Child Maintenance Service.

If the amount of maintenance you pay has been calculated by the Child Maintenance Service, this can be changed (by applying for a variation) in limited circumstances, such as if your income goes up or down by 25 per cent or more, or you pay for boarding school fees, or you have extra expenses because of a disabled child.

If you pay the flat rate because you receive certain benefits, your weekly child maintenance and any collect and pay fee can be deducted from your benefits by the DWP and sent to the Child Maintenance Service. Deductions can also be made for arrears of child maintenance, but not at the same time as deductions for ongoing weekly child maintenance. Deductions mean that your benefit will be reduced before you get it.

Further information

CPAG's *Child Support Handbook* provides detailed information about the Child Maintenance Service scheme, including calculations and enforcement

The 'get help arranging child maintenance' tool helps you compare the ways you can set up a child maintenance arrangement. You must use it if you want to apply to the Child Maintenance Service. See child-maintenance.service.gov.uk/get-help-arranging-child-maintenance

In Scotland, One Parent Families Scotland has factsheets about child maintenance and also provides a helpline for lone parents: 0808 801 0323 or see opfs.org.uk

Chapter 4
Childcare and school costs

This chapter covers:

1. **What help is available?**
2. **Is your child entitled to free childcare?**
3. **Can you get help with your childcare costs?**
4. **What other help is there before your child goes to school?**
5. **What help can you get once your child starts school?**
6. **What happens to your benefits once your child reaches school-leaving age?**

What you need to know

- Some help with childcare is free and available to all.
- Some families get extra free childcare or help to pay for childcare, depending on work, earnings or benefits.
- You may be able to get help with some school-related costs if you are on a low income. Your entitlement to help may change when your child reaches school-leaving age.

1. What help is available?

As your child gets older, support is available to help them participate in early education and childcare, such as going to pre-school, nursery or a childminder. Once your child starts school, there is also some support available to help them participate fully in school and continue in education. The support available is different in England, Scotland and Wales.

Box A

Financial help for childcare and education: checklist

- free education and childcare for two- to four-year-olds
- help from your employer
- additional amounts in universal credit
- tax-free childcare scheme
- free nursery milk for children aged under five
- Healthy Start payment card and vitamins for children aged under four in England and Wales
- Best Start and Scottish child payment in Scotland
- free school meals
- school clothing grants
- free transport to school
- childcare grant for students
- direct payments for disabled children

2. Is your child entitled to free childcare?

Some childcare and early education is available free of charge. Childcare providers must be registered. The rules vary between England, Scotland and Wales and depend on your child's age and your circumstances.

England

From 1 September 2025, if your child is at least **nine months** old, you may be entitled to 30 hours a week free childcare if you are working. If you have a partner, you must usually both be in work to qualify for this. You must each expect to earn (on average) a weekly amount equal to at least 16 hours at the national minimum wage rate for your age. There are special rules on earnings for self-employed people, so you may qualify if you earn less than this. If you or your partner are on statutory leave such as sickness, maternity, paternity or adoption leave, or one of you is unable to work because of a disability or caring responsibilities, you could still be eligible. You cannot get 30 hours free childcare if either you or your partner expect to earn £100,000 or more a year. The 30 hours free childcare can continue until your child reaches school age. You can apply online for the 30 hours free childcare at childcarechoices.gov.uk.

When your child is **two** years old, you may be entitled to 15 hours a week free childcare.

You qualify for this if you or your partner get any of the following:

- universal credit, and your take-home earnings (or joint earnings if you have a partner) are no more than £1,283.34 in the previous assessment period, or averaged over the last two or three assessment periods (£15,400 a year)
- income-related employment and support allowance
- the guarantee credit of pension credit
- asylum support

You also qualify if your child:

- is living with you while looked after by the local authority
- has a current statement of special educational needs or an education, health and care plan
- gets disability living allowance
- has left care under a special guardianship order, child arrangements order or adoption order

When your child is **three** years old, you are entitled to 15 hours a week free childcare. This childcare is available to everyone – it does not depend on your income, work or benefits. The free childcare place starts from 1 January, 1 April or 1 September following your child's third birthday, and continues until they start reception. Contact your childcare provider to claim your free childcare place.

If you qualify for 30 hours free childcare for working parents, this is the maximum available (you don't get another 15 hours free childcare on top).

The 15 or 30 hours a week is over the 38 weeks of the school year, but can be used flexibly. Apply online at childcarechoices.gov.uk.

Childcare in England must usually be registered with Ofsted.

Wales

In some areas of Wales, under the Flying Start scheme, you may be entitled to free childcare for two and a half hours a day, five days a week for 39 weeks a year from the term after your child turns **two**, and at least 15 sessions during the school holidays. The Flying Start scheme is available to children under four years old who live in some areas in Wales. Contact your local authority to find out whether you live in a Flying Start area.

Every child aged **three or four** in Wales is eligible for 10 hours' free early education each week, for 48 weeks of the year. This is known as Foundation Phase nursery. The childcare offer for Wales is 20 extra hours a week of free childcare for working parents of three- and four-year-olds for 48 weeks of the year. You qualify for that if you earn on average at least the minimum wage for 16 hours a week, and your individual gross earnings are less than £100,000 a year. Contact your local authority family information service to find out more about the support available in Wales.

Childcare in Wales must usually be registered with the Care Inspectorate Wales.

Scotland

Once your child turns **two**, you may be entitled to free childcare for 30 hours a week during term time.

You qualify for this if you or your partner get any of the following:

- universal credit and your earnings are no more than £850 in the month before you apply for the free childcare (if you have a partner, your joint earnings must be no more than £850 a month)
- income-related employment and support allowance
- pension credit
- asylum support

Your child can take up their funded childcare place from the term after their second birthday or from the term after you start receiving the qualifying benefit. Once your child becomes eligible and takes up their place, they remain entitled to a place even if your circumstances change – eg, if you no longer receive one of the above benefits.

If you are looking after a two-year-old child who is living with you under a kinship care order or a parent guardianship order, or who is looked after by the local authority, you also qualify for the free early learning and childcare place.

All children aged **three or four** are entitled to 30 hours a week (during term time) of free early learning and childcare; you do not need to be getting a benefit.

Contact your local council to find out more about free childcare.

All children entitled to a free childcare place can also get a free breakfast, lunch or dinner.

Childcare in Scotland must usually be registered with the Care Inspectorate.

3. Can you get help with your childcare costs?

If you are not covered by the free childcare provision, or need to pay for more hours, you can seek help with your childcare costs from the following sources.

- **Financial help through universal credit.** You may become entitled to universal credit once childcare costs are included.
- **Tax-free childcare.** This is a scheme in which the government tops up your contributions to a savings account specifically for paying for childcare.
- **Help from your employer.** Some employers provide their staff with a workplace nursery.

Box B

What childcare counts?

To receive help with your childcare costs, the childcare must be provided by a registered childminder, nursery, school (eg, in an out-of-school-hours club) or other approved childcare provider. You cannot get help for childcare provided by a relative, unless they are registered and the care is provided outside your home.

You can check whether a childcare provider is approved at gov.uk/help-with-childcare-costs.

Can you get help in universal credit?

When working out your entitlement to universal credit, an extra amount known as a childcare element can be included to help reimburse the cost of childcare. This is available until 1 September after your child's 16th birthday.

The amount of the childcare element is 85 per cent of your childcare costs, up to a maximum payable of £1,031.88 a month for one child and £1,768.94 a month for two or more children. The childcare must be necessary for you to work and the amount may be reduced if you claim for more childcare than is needed for you to work.

EXAMPLE

Universal credit childcare element

Yara pays £1,250 a month for childcare for her three children; 85 per cent of this is £1,062.50. This is below the maximum payable of £1,768.94 a month for two or more children, so she can be reimbursed with a childcare element of £1,062.50 a month in her universal credit.

To get the childcare element included, you must be in paid work or have an offer of paid work that is due to start shortly. There are no minimum hours. If you are in a couple, your partner must also be in paid work, unless they have limited capability for work, are caring for a severely disabled person or are temporarily absent from home. You can still get the childcare element for childcare costs while you are off work due to sickness or maternity, paternity, adoption, neonatal care or parental bereavement leave.

You should report the amount of childcare that you have paid in your online journal every month, so that your universal credit can be calculated correctly. Ask your childcare provider for receipts, as you may need to provide evidence or upload copies to your online journal. You can report the amount you have paid in the following month and it will be included, or up to 13 months after you have paid the costs if you are accepted as having a good reason for not reporting them earlier.

You can get help with the childcare charges you have paid in the month before starting work, including a deposit, registration fee or advance charges. You can continue to get help with childcare costs in the month after stopping work.

If you owe your childcare provider for childcare provided in a previous month, the amount included in your universal credit can cover payments you have made towards your arrears (subject to the monthly limit).

If you need to pay childcare costs so that you can start work, but cannot afford to pay until you receive the help from universal credit at the end of your monthly assessment period, you can ask your work coach to access the Flexible Support Fund, which can be used to pay your first month's childcare fees. This is a discretionary payment which does not have to be paid back, and you can still get 85 per cent of your total costs (subject to the monthly limit) reimbursed at the end of your monthly assessment period. If you cannot get help from the Flexible Support Fund, you can ask for a budgeting advance of universal credit. See Chapter 11 for details.

Tax-free childcare

If your income is too high for universal credit, you may be able to get some help through tax-free childcare. The government contributes £2 for every £8 you pay into a savings account reserved for paying your registered childcare provider.

The childcare must be for a child aged under 12, or 17 if they are disabled. You must be working and earning at least the rate of the national minimum wage appropriate for your age for a 16-hour week, and no more than £100,000 a year.

You can get up to £2,000 a year top-up for each child, or up to £4,000 for a disabled child.

What CPAG says

Tax-free childcare

Tax-free childcare may appear to have some advantages, but could leave you worse off if you are on a low income. You cannot get help through tax-free childcare if you are getting universal credit or childcare vouchers from your employer. If you apply for tax-free childcare, you cannot get any universal credit at the same time (not just the help with childcare costs). As universal credit includes amounts for basic needs as well as childcare, you will usually be much worse off on the tax-free childcare scheme.

Note: the scheme does not have anything directly to do with tax. You can find more information, and a link for applying, at gov.uk/get-tax-free-childcare.

Can you get help from your employer?

Some employers provide workplace nurseries. You do not have to pay tax or national insurance on this childcare.

Some employees may still be receiving help from their employer through childcare vouchers or directly contracted childcare, but these schemes closed to new applicants in 2018.

Childcare grant for students

If you are a full-time student with a child aged under 15, or 17 if they have special educational needs, you may be eligible for a childcare grant in England and Wales to help with costs of registered childcare. In Scotland, if you are a student with a child, you may be able to get help from the discretionary childcare fund. Ask your college or university for more information.

Direct payments for disabled children

If your local authority has assessed your child as needing care and support services, you can ask to be paid directly for the costs of these services so that you can buy them yourself instead of getting services from the local authority. Ask your local authority for more information.

4. What other help is there before your child goes to school?

Free nursery milk

If your child is under five years old and is in registered childcare or early education for two hours or more a day, they are entitled to about a third of a pint of milk each day. The milk can be any pasteurised cow's milk, including whole, semi-skimmed and organic. Fully skimmed milk, goat's milk, soya milk, lactose-free milk, fluoridated milk, unpasteurised milk or milk with added flavours, colours, vitamins or other additives are not included. Babies under one are allowed fresh milk or specified brands of infant formula milk. In Scotland, alternatives are available for children who cannot drink cow's milk for medical, ethical or religious reasons, and your child is also entitled to one healthy snack a day, which includes fresh fruit, vegetables or mixed fruit.

Healthy Start payment card and vitamins

You continue to get credits on your payment card for milk, fruit and vegetables and free vitamins from the Healthy Start scheme while your child is under four, whether or not they are in early education or childcare or receiving free nursery milk. Chapter 2 has more details on the scheme.

Best Start and Scottish child payment in Scotland

In Scotland, the Best Start foods payment card can continue until your child turns three. You can apply for the Best Start grant early learning payment in Scotland from when your child is aged two to three and a half, and the school age payment from 1 June in the year they are able to start school. You can apply for Scottish child payment at any time for a child under the age of 16. Chapter 2 has more details on these schemes.

Free lunches in Scotland

In Scotland, children who qualify for free childcare or early education from age two are also entitled to a free lunch at their pre-school nursery.

5. What help can you get once your child starts school?

When your child starts school, you may find that there are unexpected costs connected to their education. As well as things like school uniforms and basic equipment, there may be other equipment, activities or trips that involve some additional spending. It is important that your child is able to participate fully in school, so make sure you are getting everything you are entitled to and not missing out on support.

What families say

School costs

'School trips are definitely not affordable now my children are in high school... I feel so ashamed and sad that my kids don't even ask me if they can go because by myself the answer is always no, it's just simply not an option for me currently or even in their lifetime of being at school.' *Gracie E, Changing Realities*

Free school meals

Once your child starts school, they may be entitled to a free school meal (lunch). At some stages, free school meals are available to everyone; at other stages they are only for children in households on low incomes. The rules vary between England, Scotland and Wales and depend on your child's age and your circumstances. The following rules are the legal minimum, but local authorities can extend free school meals to other groups, so check the policy in your area.

If your child is entitled to free school meals due to your income, you may qualify for other help, such as a school clothing grant or free school holiday activities and food. So, in order not to miss out on any possible support, it is important to apply for free school meals even while your child is in the stages of primary school when all children are eligible for them.

There are local pilot schemes and plans to expand free school meals to more children throughout the UK.

England

All children in reception, year 1 and year 2 are entitled to free school meals.

Otherwise, your child is entitled to free school meals if you get any of the following:

- universal credit, and your earnings (or joint earnings if you have a partner) are no more than £616.67 a month (this works out as

£7,400 a year, and can be averaged over the last two or three months) – with no earnings limit from September 2026
- income-related employment and support allowance
- the guarantee credit of pension credit
- asylum support

Your child is also entitled to free school meals if you are excluded from benefits due to immigration status but your income is within certain limits.

If you are on a low income but do not fall into any of these categories, your local authority may provide free school meals on a discretionary basis or under a pilot scheme to expand entitlement. For example, all primary school children in Greater London can get free school meals.

Wales

All children in primary school are entitled to free school meals, and can also access free school breakfasts.

Otherwise, your child is entitled to free school meals if you get any of the following:

- universal credit, and your earnings (or joint earnings if you have a partner) are no more than £616.67 a month (this works out as £7,400 a year, and can be averaged over the last two or three months)
- income-related employment and support allowance
- the guarantee credit of pension credit
- asylum support

If you are on a low income but do not fall into any of these categories, for example because you are excluded from benefits due to immigration status, your local authority may provide free school meals on a discretionary basis.

Scotland

All children in primary 1 to 5 are entitled to free school meals.

Children in primary 6 and 7 are entitled to free school meals if you get Scottish child payment.

Otherwise, your child is entitled to free school meals if you get any of the following:

- universal credit, and your earnings (or joint earnings if you have a partner) are no more than £850 a month
- income-related employment and support allowance
- asylum support

If you are on a low income but do not fall into any of these categories, for example because you get pension credit or you are excluded from benefits due to immigration status, your local authority may provide free school meals on a discretionary basis.

Help in the school holidays

If your child qualifies for free school meals due to your income, you may be able to get additional help during the school holidays. Local authorities may provide holiday activities and food, or can make payments to the equivalent value of school meals.

School clothing grant

You may qualify for a grant to help buy school uniforms and other school clothing. There are schemes in Scotland and Wales. Each local authority in England sets its own qualifying conditions, but you usually qualify if you receive one of the benefits that qualify you for free school meals. Some schools also provide other help, such as uniform exchange schemes.

School transport

If you live more than a certain distance from your nearest suitable school, or there is no safe walking route, local authorities must provide your child with free transport to school if it is considered necessary.

Free school transport may also be provided if your child has special educational needs or if you are on a low income – eg, if you qualify for free school meals.

6. What happens to your benefits when your child reaches school-leaving age?

You can continue to get child benefit and amounts in your universal credit for your child (the child element) until 1 September after their 16th birthday – even if they leave school, or are unable to attend school for any reason. Payments can also continue after 1 September if they stay on at school or go to college, provided the course they are doing is full time and non-advanced or if it is an approved training course. If this is the case, your child benefit continues until their 20th birthday. The child element in your universal credit continues for a young person in non-advanced education until 1 September after their 19th birthday.

Box C

What is full-time, non-advanced education and approved training?

Full time means, on average, at least 12 hours a week during term time, including tuition, supervised study, exams and practical work, but not including meal breaks and unsupervised study. The course must normally be provided by a school or college. If your child is home-schooled, this can count if it began before the age of 16, or if it started after the age of 16 because of a disability.

Non-advanced courses include GCSEs, A levels and Scottish Highers, but not a university degree or a diploma.

Approved training. In England, training must count as appropriate full-time education, which means it is suitable for the young person's age, ability and aptitude, and any special educational needs. In Wales, training must be a Traineeship or Foundation Apprenticeship or Jobs Growth Wales+. In Scotland, training must be provided under the No One Left Behind scheme. A training course does not count as approved training if it is provided as part of a job.

You can still get child benefit if there is a reason why your child is temporarily unable to continue in education – for up to six months for some reasons, or indefinitely if it is due to an illness or disability.

You can continue to claim child benefit for a 16/17-year-old who has left full-time, non-advanced education or approved training, provided they have registered for work or training with the careers service. This period can continue for up to 20 weeks and you must report this within three months of the date they left education.

You cannot continue to claim in this period if they start work for 24 hours or more a week.

You can continue to get child benefit and universal credit for a young person aged 19, but they must have started, enrolled or been accepted on the course before turning 19. You can only get an amount for them in your universal credit until 1 September after their 19th birthday.

Make sure you tell the relevant office that deals with your child benefit and universal credit if your child is staying on in full-time, non-advanced education or approved training after school-leaving age. Contact each office separately as you cannot rely on them sharing information. You should tell them each August/September whether your child is continuing in education, and if they change courses at any time during the year.

You should also report if your child is not living with you for any reason. Even if your child is living with you and continuing in full-time, non-advanced education, there are some situations in which you cannot continue to claim child benefit and universal credit for them.

You cannot claim benefit for a young person if they are married or living with their partner as a couple and their partner is not in full-time, non-advanced education or approved training. This is the case, even if they are both living with you.

You cannot claim for a young person if they claim universal credit, jobseeker's allowance or employment and support allowance in their own right. Sometimes, you may be able to choose whether to continue claiming child benefit and universal credit for your child once they have reached school-leaving age, or whether they would be better off claiming universal credit in their own right.

Is there any other help for young people in education?

If your child is between 16 and 19 and continuing in full-time, non-advanced education in Scotland or Wales, they may be able to claim an education maintenance allowance, depending on your household income. The education maintenance allowance is £40 a week in Wales and £30 a week in Scotland.

In England, your child may be able to get help with their studies from the 16 to 19 bursary fund, depending on the circumstances. A bursary for students in vulnerable situations, such as being care experienced or without parental support or having a disability, is payable at up to £1,200 a year.

Discretionary bursaries may also be available from schools and colleges in England, Scotland and Wales.

If your child has moved on to full-time, advanced education (university degree level), they will usually have to rely on student loans and any other discretionary grants available. See CPAG's *Student Support and Benefits Handbook* and *Benefits for Students in Scotland Handbook* for more information about when other help may be available.

Further information

You can find more information on government support with childcare in England, Wales and Scotland at childcarechoices.gov.uk

For more information on childcare in Scotland, contact your local authority Family Information Service or see parentclub.scot

Find your local Family Information Service in Wales at gov.wales/find-your-local-family-information-service

For an official calculator to help work out what help you can get with childcare costs, see gov.uk/childcare-calculator

Chapter 5
Being out of work or working on a low income

This chapter covers:

What you need to know

- Benefits are available to help with your basic needs in a number of situations, including if you are looking for work, if you are in work on a low income, if you are unable to work because you are ill or have a disability, or if you have caring responsibilities. Universal credit depends on how much money you have coming in; some other benefits depend on your national insurance contribution record.
- In most cases, in order to get benefit, you must meet certain responsibilities related to work, such as attending interviews with the DWP and undergoing retraining in order to increase your chances of finding a job.
- Extra support for being unable to work because of illness or disability involves an official assessment of your capability for work.

1. What help is available?

If you are not in paid work, or if you are but your income is low, you may be able to claim social security benefits to help you meet your family's basic needs. You may be in one of the following situations.

- You may not be working because you are at home looking after your new baby or young children.
- You may have lost your job and are currently looking for work.
- You may be working, either part time or full time, but your earnings are insufficient to cover your costs.
- You may have a health condition or disability that limits your ability to work, or you may be off work because you are ill.
- You may be a carer for a disabled person (see Chapter 7).

You may be able to claim universal credit to help top up your income. You may be able to claim jobseeker's allowance or employment and support allowance, depending on your national insurance record, to provide an income instead of earnings. You must meet certain rules related to work. These are outlined in this chapter.

This chapter covers the rules for working-age benefits. If you are over pension age, you do not have any work-related requirements. If you are getting pension credit and working, your earnings are taken into account after a fixed weekly amount is disregarded.

Box A

Financial help while you are out of work or working on a low income: checklist

- universal credit
- jobseeker's allowance
- statutory sick pay
- industrial injuries benefits
- employment and support allowance

Universal credit can also help with your rent. Chapter 6 has more about help with housing costs. If you are on a low income, you may also get help with paying your council tax (council tax reduction).

You can also claim child benefit. Chapter 2 has more about this.

2. Are you looking after a young child?

You do not have to look for work while you are responsible for a baby or a child under the age of three, but you can if you want to.

If you claim universal credit, you do not have to look for work until your child is aged three. You can get universal credit if you are a lone parent or part of a couple. If you are part of a couple on universal credit, you and your partner should decide between you who you want to nominate as the responsible carer for your child(ren). This can only be changed once in the following 12 months or if there has been a change in your circumstances, such as if one of you has stopped or started work. The following rules apply if you get universal credit.

- While your baby is under the age of one, you do not have any work-related requirements.
- While your child is aged one, you are usually required to attend work-focused interviews to discuss your future employability options. These are at least every three months, but may be more frequently. You can bring your child with you to the interview or request a payment for childcare costs, if this is not suitable. You should participate in the interviews but you do not need to agree to any follow-up action. Your universal credit may be sanctioned if you fail to attend the interview without a good reason.
- While your child is aged two, you are usually required to attend work-focused interviews every month and undertake some activity to prepare for work, such as preparing a CV or attending skills training. If you need help with childcare costs to participate, ask your work coach. Your universal credit may be sanctioned if you refuse to undertake activity without a good reason. You do not have to look for work yet.

- When your child turns three, you are expected to look for work, usually for up to 30 hours a week. You need to agree to be available for work, depending on suitable childcare being available. Your universal credit may be sanctioned if you refuse to look for work or take up a job without good reason.

If you claim jobseeker's allowance, you must look for work as agreed, whatever the age of your child.

3. Are you looking for work?

You usually have to look for work:

- if you are a lone parent with a child aged three or over
- if you are part of a couple and your partner is the lead carer for a child under three
- (as does your partner) when your youngest child reaches the age of three

If you are looking for work, the key benefits for meeting your and your family's basic needs are jobseeker's allowance and universal credit.

If you have worked in the past and paid enough national insurance contributions, you may be able to get jobseeker's allowance. This is only paid for a maximum of 182 days. Otherwise, you may be able to get universal credit.

You can be paid jobseeker's allowance at the same time as universal credit, but your universal credit is reduced by the amount of your jobseeker's allowance.

To get jobseeker's allowance or universal credit while looking for work, you must accept a claimant commitment and fulfil certain responsibilities related to work.

You may also be able to get jobseeker's allowance if you are doing some part-time work. You can also get universal credit while you are working – there are no limits on the amount of work you can do.

4. Are you in paid work?

If you are in paid work, but your income is low, you may be able to claim universal credit to top up your earnings.

If you are not working, or only working a few hours a week, you may be able to get jobseeker's allowance, depending on your national insurance record, and/or universal credit to help top up your income.

What families say

In-work poverty

'My income used to be different amounts when I was on UC. Some months I wouldn't get anything and this left me having to use foodbanks, etc. I then took a second job to stabilise my income. Recently my wage was lower as I have been put on a different tax banding due to having two jobs. This meant my income was £200 less despite working the same hours, etc. I don't know what else to do as I can't physically work any more hours.' *Pammy W, Changing Realities*

Universal credit

What are the rules about work?

Universal credit is a benefit for people on a low income who are in paid work, as well as for people who are out of work. There are no rules about the amount of work you can or must do – you can claim universal credit even if you work full time or only a few hours each week. However, to get universal credit, even if you are working, you must accept a claimant commitment in which you agree to do certain things in return for receiving benefit (known as your work-related requirements).

If you only work part time and your earnings are low, you may have to be available and looking for more work. This could be working more hours in your current job or working more hours (or earning more) in another job. However, once your earnings reach a certain level, you no longer need to be available for more work or to look for more work. The amount of this threshold is equivalent to the national minimum wage for someone of your age for the number of hours you are expected to work. If you are aged at least 21 and your child is at least three years old and under 13, this is usually 30 hours a week, and your threshold works out as £1,587 a month as a single person. If you have a partner, their threshold is usually 35 hours a week, which works out as £1,851 a month; this is added to yours and your joint earnings are considered.

If your earnings are below this threshold but you are earning at least the equivalent of 18 hours a week at the minimum wage (£952 a month) as a single person or 29 hours a week (£1,534 a month) if you are in a couple, you do not have to look for more work. You may still be required to attend work-focused interviews or take action to help you obtain more work or better-paid work.

How are your earnings assessed?

The amount of universal credit you get depends on your income, so your earnings are taken into account, together with any other income you have that affects your entitlement – eg, certain benefits, including jobseeker's allowance, employment and support allowance and carer's allowance, and income from a pension.

Your earnings include your basic wages, as well as any overtime, holiday pay, sick pay and tax rebates. They also include payments from your employer – eg, statutory sick pay or contractual sick pay, statutory maternity pay and statutory paternity pay.

Your earnings are assessed on a monthly basis. If you are employed, you need to check the amount of your earnings as shown on your online journal each month, which is automatically obtained from your employer when you are paid – this is called real-time information.

Your net earnings are used – ie, after deductions for income tax, class 1 national insurance contributions and any contribution you make towards a personal or occupational pension scheme.

If you are self-employed, you must report your profits every month. Profits are worked out by deducting permitted expenses from your receipts. These can include things like rent, wages and insurance, purchase of equipment and stock, and VAT. If you have been self-employed and claiming universal credit for over a year, and your earnings are low, your universal credit may be based on higher earnings than you actually have. This is called the minimum income floor and, if your child is under 13, is usually set at 30 hours a week at the minimum wage; a monthly take-home amount of approximately £1,435 if you are 21 or over.

People with children can earn up to a certain level without losing any universal credit. This is called a work allowance. This is £411 a month if your universal credit includes housing costs, or £684 a month if it does not. If your (and your partner's combined) earnings are less than the work allowance, your universal credit is not reduced at all. If earnings are more than the work allowance, your universal credit is reduced by 55 per cent of the amount above the allowance.

EXAMPLE

Assessing earnings for universal credit

Gemma is a lone parent with a child aged six. Her universal credit includes an amount to help with her rent. She has a part-time job, earning £600 a month. Gemma qualifies for a work allowance of £411 a month when her universal credit is calculated. Gemma's earnings exceed her work allowance by £189 (£600 – £411). So the amount of Gemma's earnings taken into account as income for universal credit is 55 per cent of £189 = £103.95.

Jobseeker's allowance

What are the rules about work?

Jobseeker's allowance is a benefit based on national insurance contributions. It is for people who are unemployed and looking for work, but you can also be entitled while doing some part-time work and looking for more work. It is usually known as new-style jobseeker's allowance. You must have previously been employed and paying national insurance contributions to qualify.

You must either be unemployed or working less than 16 hours a week. If you have a partner, it does not matter how much work they do.

To get jobseeker's allowance, even if you are working, you must accept a claimant commitment in which you agree to do certain things in return for receiving benefit (known as your work-related requirements).

How are your earnings assessed?

The amount of jobseeker's allowance you get is reduced by certain types of income.

Your earnings are assessed on a weekly basis after £5 a week is disregarded.

Your net earnings are taken into account. Your net earnings are your earnings after deductions for income tax, class 1 national insurance contributions and half of any contribution you make towards a personal or occupational pension scheme. The amount of any such pension over £50 a week is also taken into account.

5. What are your responsibilities?

Most people must satisfy certain work-related responsibilities to get jobseeker's allowance and universal credit. The requirements that apply to you depend on your circumstances. You can negotiate about these with your work coach at the job centre. If they agree, you can, for instance, place limitations on the work you are looking for – eg, the type of work, its location, the number of hours and the rate of pay.

If you do not carry out your requirements, you may be sanctioned and your benefit reduced. The sanctions can be severe, so you should always try to avoid one if you can.

What families say

Sanctions

'[T]here was no empathy or understanding for my child being unwell when it came to appointments. I phoned the job centre to change appt time to be told if I did not attend my benefits would be sanctioned. My daughter has chickenpox and ear infection. I had to take a bus and carry a 6 year old into the job centre. She is autistic and cried loudly through the appt. The advisor was abrupt and asked why I didn't leave her with a family member.' *Bessie J, Changing Realities*

What CPAG says

Avoiding a sanction

- If you cannot attend or you miss a work-focused interview, contact your work coach as soon as possible to explain why.
- Does your claimant commitment take into account your childcare responsibilities and any difficulties you have in looking for work? Make sure your work coach or personal adviser is aware of these and ask that they be taken into account.
- If you are finding it hard to carry out all the responsibilities in your claimant commitment, ask for it to be reviewed.
- If your circumstances change, tell your work coach straight away; your claimant commitment may also need changing.
- Keep a written record of everything you do to look for, or prepare for, work.
- If you do not think that an activity or course is suitable for you, let your work coach know and ask not to take part in it.
- Try to stick to your claimant commitment, but if you have a good reason for not keeping to it (eg, because you have been ill), let your work coach know as soon as possible.

A sanction should not be applied if you have a good reason for your actions. If you are given a sanction, you can challenge it. Chapter 11 has more information on this.

Accepting a claimant commitment

For jobseeker's allowance and universal credit, you must accept a claimant commitment. This is a written record of what you must do in return for your benefit (your responsibilities and work-related requirements). If you do not accept a claimant commitment, you are not entitled to benefit, unless there are exceptional circumstances – eg, if you cannot act for yourself or you have a domestic emergency.

Box B
Your claimant commitment

- Your claimant commitment is drawn up with your work coach at the job centre. It can be completed online, by phone or in person.
- The commitment is a record of the responsibilities you must fulfil in order to get benefit – eg, what you must do to look for work and what your pattern of availability for work is. It also records how you will be sanctioned and your benefit reduced if you do not meet your responsibilities.
- Make sure you tell your work coach about any problems you have with looking for work and tell them what limitations you have.
- If you are unhappy with your claimant commitment, you can ask for it to be reviewed at any time. However, because you must accept a claimant commitment in order to get benefit, it is best to accept it first and then ask for it to be reviewed at a later date.

What are the work-related requirements for universal credit?

- **Attending work-focused interviews**. These are interviews, usually at the job centre, about your work prospects, and any training, education and rehabilitation that might help you.
- **Work preparation**. This is particular action that you may be required to take to be better prepared for work, such as going to a skills presentation or taking part in an employment programme.
- **Work search**. This means taking all reasonable action to look for work, regardless of the type of work or salary. You are usually expected to spend 30 hours a week looking for work while your child is aged at least three and under 13. If you have a disability or are caring for someone with a disability, these hours can be fewer. You are usually expected to look for work in locations up to 90 minutes' travel time from your home.
- **Work availability**. You must be able and willing to take up paid work (including more or better-paid work) immediately. This requirement can be eased if you are doing voluntary work and need longer notice, if you have caring responsibilities that require you to be given more time, or if you are already working and must give your employer notice that you are leaving the job. You must also be willing and able to attend a job interview immediately. You are usually expected to be available for work of at least 30 hours a week while your child is aged at least three and under 13. These hours may be fewer if you have a disability or are caring for someone with a disability.

What families say

Work availability

'Decisions being made [this year] about what I can give to a career. How can I manage both a career and my caring role which sees me driving over a hundred miles a week for my son, hanging around... whilst [he] has a session? It's restrictive and it does impact availability a lot.' *Evelyn D, Changing Realities*

Some people must meet all the work-related requirements. You have fewer requirements placed on you if you have a child, but the requirements increase as your child reaches their first, second and third birthdays.

If you are in a couple, only one of you can have fewer requirements placed on you because you have a child. This is the partner who is the child's main carer. You count as the child's main carer if you and your partner have nominated you.

If your youngest child is aged at least three but under 13, you only have to look for and be available for work during their normal childcare or school hours (including travelling time to and from childcare provider or school), usually 30 hours a week during term time. You do not have to accept a job which would mean having to leave them on their own after school.

If your child is aged at least 13 and under 16, you are usually expected to be available and looking for work for 35 hours a week, but this can be reduced, depending on the needs of your child.

If you are home-schooling your child, there is no special provision made to your work-related requirements, unless this is in an emergency because the school is closed.

Your work-related requirements can be lifted temporarily at your work coach's discretion – eg, if your child is ill or has been suspended from school.

EXAMPLE

Universal credit work-related requirements

Ghita and Sanjay are not working and have a baby, Kapil. They claim universal credit. Ghita is Kapil's main carer and does not need to look for work, be available for work or attend interviews about work. When Kapil reaches one year old, Ghita may have to attend work-focused interviews.

Sanjay must look for work and be available for work and job interviews.

Which work-related requirements apply?

People with children	
You are pregnant and there are 11 weeks or less before your baby is due, or you had a baby not more than 15 weeks ago.	No requirements.
You have a child under one year old, or you have adopted a child within the previous 12 months.	No requirements.
Your youngest child is one year old.	Work-focused interviews only, usually every three months.
Your youngest child is two years old.	Work-focused interviews, usually every month, and work preparation.
Your youngest child is at least three years old and under 13.	Work-focused interviews, work preparation, work search and work availability, usually for 30 hours a week.
Your youngest child is at least 13 years old.	Work-focused interviews, work preparation, work search and work availability, usually for 35 hours a week.
You are a foster parent of a child under one year old.	No requirements.
You are a foster parent of a child aged between one and 16 years old.	Work-focused interviews only; this can also apply after the age of 16 and to your partner if the child has care needs which make it unreasonable to expect you to do more.
You have experienced domestic abuse.	No requirements for 13 weeks from when you notify the DWP. If you have a child under 16, you are allowed a further 13 weeks with no work search or work availability requirements. See Chapter 10 for more information.

Which work-related requirements apply?	
Other situations	
You are caring for a severely disabled person for at least 35 hours a week.	No requirements.
You have a severe health condition or disability and have limited capability for work-related activity.	No requirements.
You have a significant health condition or disability and have limited capability for work.	Work-focused interviews and work preparation only.
You are working and your earnings are at least the sum of the minimum wage multiplied by your expected hours of work.	No requirements.
You are working and you are earning at least a set amount (at the time of writing, £952 a month if you are single or £1,534 a month if you are in a couple).	Work-focused interviews and work preparation only.
You are working and your partner or child has died within the last six months, or you are looking after a child and a death, violence or abuse has significantly disrupted your life in the last two years.	Work-focused interviews and work preparation only.

What are the jobseeking conditions for jobseeker's allowance?

Being available for work. You must usually be willing and able to take up work immediately, at any time, and to take a job of at least 40 hours a week (although you must also be prepared to work part time). You can be allowed more time if you are doing voluntary work (or providing some other service), if you have caring responsibilities, or if you are working part time and must give your employer notice that you are leaving your job.

If you are a lone parent with a child under 13 years old, you can restrict your availability to your child's usual school hours, usually 30 hours a week during term time.

If you have a child under 16 years old, or are looking after someone with a disability or someone over pension age, you can be available for less than 40 hours' work a week, provided you are available to work at least 16 hours and you have a reasonable chance of getting work.

You do not have to be available for work in some situations. These include if there is a domestic emergency (eg, if one of your children is ill), or if you have experienced domestic violence and you have told the DWP of this within the last four weeks.

Actively seeking work. You are usually expected to take at least three steps each week to ensure you have the best prospects of getting work. Keep a record of what you have done. Steps can include:

- applying for jobs
- seeking information about jobs
- registering with an employment agency
- preparing your CV
- making enquiries about jobs via the internet or email

6. Are you unable to work because you are sick or disabled?

If you are unable to work because you are sick or you have a long-term health condition or disability, you may be able to get benefit to help meet your basic needs. See Chapter 7 for further help you may be able to get.

Are you employed?

If you are employed but are incapable of doing your job because you are sick or you have a long-term health condition or disability, you may be able to get statutory sick pay from your employer. To qualify, you must have been earning enough to pay national insurance contributions. You cannot get statutory sick pay if you are entitled to statutory maternity pay or maternity allowance, or if you are self-employed.

Statutory sick pay is paid by your employer for a maximum of 28 weeks.

You may also be entitled to contractual sick pay from your employer. This depends on the terms of your contract. If you are entitled to contractual sick pay, your employer can deduct your statutory sick pay from your contractual sick pay.

If you are on a low income, your statutory sick pay (and contractual sick pay) can be topped up by universal credit.

If you are employed and disabled as a result of an accident at work or a disease caused by your job, you may be entitled to industrial injuries benefits. This does not apply if you are self-employed. To be entitled, you must have been injured in an industrial accident or have a prescribed industrial disease, and be assessed as being sufficiently disabled.

What if you do not get statutory sick pay?

If you are not entitled to statutory sick pay (including because you are not employed) or if you have received your full 28 weeks' entitlement and are still unable to work, you may be able to get employment and support allowance and/or universal credit. If you have worked in the past and paid enough national insurance contributions, you may be able to get employment and support allowance. This is usually known as new-style employment and support allowance. Employment and support allowance can be topped up by universal credit.

If you have received your full entitlement to statutory sick pay, your employer should give you Form SSP1 to support your claim for employment and support allowance. You can get employment and support allowance even if you are still employed, but not if you have returned to work of 16 hours or more a week, or are earning more than £195.50 a week. If you work less than 16 hours and do not earn more than £195.50 a week, you can still get employment and support allowance in full. It is reduced by 50 per cent of a private or occupational pension over £85 a week.

If you cannot get employment and support allowance because you do not have enough national insurance contributions, you may still be able to get universal credit.

How is your ability to work assessed?

In order to get employment and support allowance, you must have what is known as limited capability for work. If you get universal credit, having limited capability for work means that your work-related requirements are reduced and you may get extra support.

You must first provide a medical certificate from your doctor. You will then usually have to have a work capability assessment. This means that you must complete a questionnaire about your health and attend a medical examination. If you fail to return the questionnaire or miss the medical without a good reason, you are automatically treated as being fit for work.

Information from your doctor, the questionnaire and the medical examination is used to decide whether you score sufficient points to count as having limited capability for work. Some people, including people who have a terminal illness or are receiving chemotherapy or radiotherapy for cancer, automatically pass the assessment.

In exceptional circumstances, you can be treated as having limited capability for work even though you would not otherwise be. The most common of these situations is where there would be a substantial risk to your health (or to someone else's health) if you had to work, look for work or (if your condition is severe) do work-related activity.

You are automatically treated as having limited capability for work if you are pregnant and there is a serious risk to your health or to your baby's health if you work.

You are automatically treated as having limited capability for work for employment and support allowance if you are pregnant and entitled to maternity allowance, if you are within six weeks of the expected date of the birth or you are within 14 days of having given birth.

For employment and support allowance, if you are waiting for an assessment to be carried out, you can be treated as having limited capability for work and so get benefit while your medical examination is being arranged, provided you have submitted a medical certificate. However, if you are reclaiming after having already failed the assessment and your health condition has not changed or significantly deteriorated, this does not apply.

For universal credit, you are not treated as having limited capability for work while you are waiting for an assessment to be carried out. You can still get universal credit while you are waiting to be assessed, but you may be required to look for work. However, your work coach has the discretion to waive this requirement in this situation, in particular if you have submitted a medical certificate and they consider it is unreasonable to expect you to look for work.

What are your work-related requirements?

Even though you have limited capability for work, to get your full entitlement of employment and support allowance you must still attend work-focused interviews and undertake work-related activity, such as preparing a CV or basic skills training. You cannot be required to apply for a job or do any work, but you can agree to do work experience or voluntary work.

To get universal credit, you must still accept a claimant commitment and to get your full entitlement, you must usually attend work-focused interviews and prepare for work. This is activity intended to make it more likely that you will return to work. The requirements must be reasonable and take all your circumstances into account.

However, as well as assessing your ability to work, the work capability assessment also looks at whether you have what the law calls limited capability for work-related activity. This is whether you are so ill or disabled that you cannot be expected to attend work-focused interviews, undertake work-related activity or prepare for work.

Your responsibilities may also be affected by your other circumstances, including if you have a young child. You do not have any work-related responsibilities if you are a lone parent with a child under one year old. For employment and support allowance, you continue not to have any work-related responsibilities while your youngest child is aged under three. For universal credit and employment and support allowance, your work-related requirements start to increase when your youngest child turns one.

If you get carer's allowance for looking after a disabled person, you do not have any work-related responsibilities.

If you fail to take part in an interview or refuse to undertake work-related activity without a good reason, you may be sanctioned. This means the amount of your employment and support allowance or universal credit is reduced until you comply. Good reason is not defined, but all your circumstances should be taken into account, including your illness, disability, caring responsibilities, language and transport problems. If you have been sanctioned, you can challenge this. See Chapter 11 for more information.

Further information

For more information about universal credit, sanctions and conditionality, go to cpag.org.uk/welfare-rights

You can find full details about limited capability for work and the work capability assessment in CPAG's *Welfare Benefits Handbook*

Chapter 6
Housing costs

This chapter covers:

1. What help is available?
2. Do you pay rent?
3. Are you paying a mortgage?
4. Can you get a discretionary housing payment?
5. Can you get help with your council tax?
6. Can you get help with heating costs?

What you need to know

- If you are on a low income, you may be able to get help with your rent through universal credit or, sometimes, housing benefit.
- You may be able to get a loan to help with your mortgage if you get universal credit or pension credit.
- You may be eligible to pay a reduced amount of council tax due to your circumstances or low income.
- You may be eligible for help with your heating costs.

1. What help is available?

If you have a low income, you may be able to get help with your rent, mortgage payments, council tax and heating costs. This chapter explains what help is available.

Box A

Financial help for housing costs: checklist

- universal credit for rent or service charges for owner-occupiers
- housing benefit for rent in some circumstances, or if you are over pension age
- pension credit for service charges for owner-occupiers, if you are over pension age
- discretionary housing payments for rent
- support for mortgage interest loans for owner-occupiers
- council tax reduction
- winter fuel payment (in England and Wales)
- cold weather payment (in England and Wales)
- pension age winter heating payment (in Scotland)
- winter heating payment (in Scotland)
- child winter heating payment (in Scotland)

2. Do you pay rent?

If you are on a low income, you may be able to get universal credit, which includes a housing costs element to help with paying your rent and certain service charges. You can get help whether you are in or out of work, and as a council, housing association or private landlord tenant.

You can get help with the rent on the home in which you normally live. In limited situations, you can get help with two properties – eg, if you had to move because of a fear of domestic abuse.

Housing benefit for people who are under pension age has been replaced by universal credit. You cannot get housing benefit in a standard tenancy and must claim universal credit instead. There are exceptions: if you live in a certain type of temporary homeless accommodation or specified supported housing accommodation, such as a domestic abuse refuge, you can claim housing benefit, rather than universal credit, to help with rent.

How much help could you get?

The amount you get towards your rent in universal credit and housing benefit depends on all your circumstances, including the amount of income and savings you have, the size of your household and the size and type of property you rent.

Box B

Special rules if you are affected by domestic abuse

See Chapter 10 if you are affected by domestic abuse.

- If you are staying in a refuge, you claim housing benefit for your rent, not universal credit.
- You may be able to get help with rent on two homes for up to 12 months if you have moved because of a fear of abuse or violence, and if you intend to return to your normal home.
- If your home is a sanctuary scheme adapted home provided by a local authority or housing association, your rent is not reduced if you have too many bedrooms; you will need to provide evidence of the abuse from someone like a social worker or a domestic abuse organisation staff member.

Do you live in a privately rented home?

If you have a private landlord, the amount you get in universal credit or pension-age housing benefit is limited to a set figure, the local housing allowance. The figures, or rates, are usually set annually for the size of property you are assessed as needing. Each local authority has its own rates for properties up to a maximum of four bedrooms. You can check these at lha-direct.voa.gov.uk.

If you are living in a property considered too big for you and your family, not all your rent is covered. If you are in rent arrears or facing eviction because of the shortfall, get advice.

You are allowed one bedroom for each of the following:

- a couple
- someone aged 16 or over who is not a lodger

- two children aged under 16 of the same sex
- two children aged under 10
- any other child aged under 16
- a carer/carers providing overnight care for a disabled child or adult

You may be allowed an additional bedroom if, for example, your child has a disability which means they cannot share a bedroom with a sibling, you are a couple but cannot share a room because of a disability, or if you are a foster carer. There are special rules for students and members of the armed forces, who may qualify for a bedroom even if they do not live in your home all of the time.

EXAMPLE

Local housing allowance

Flora lives with her son aged 10 and her two daughters aged five and two in a three-bedroom private rented flat. The rent is £800 a month. She gets universal credit. The local housing allowance rules allow one bedroom for Flora, one for her son and one for her daughters. The allowance for a three-bedroom property in her area is £750 a month. Flora gets a housing costs element in her universal credit of £750 a month, and has a rent shortfall.

Do you live in a council or housing association home?

If you live in a council/local authority/housing association property, the help you can get with your rent in universal credit can be similarly restricted, commonly called the bedroom tax. The bedroom tax does not apply if you are getting housing benefit because you are over pension age, or in temporary homeless or exempt supported accommodation.

The number of bedrooms you are allowed is calculated in the same way as for private rented property. If you have one more bedroom than you are allowed, the amount of rent covered by your benefit is reduced by 14 per cent. If you have two or more additional bedrooms, it is reduced by 25 per cent.

What families say

Bedroom tax

'Our client splits the care for her son equally with the child's dad. As dad gets the child element on his universal credit, he is considered the one responsible for their son. Because of this, mum is subject to the bedroom tax and has her benefits reduced despite her son using the bedroom for half the week.' *Foodbank welfare rights adviser, Early Warning System*

If your universal credit is reduced in this way, you should apply for a discretionary housing payment from the local authority. While this is discretionary, in Scotland there is a commitment to cover shortfalls due to the bedroom tax, so they should always be met.

EXAMPLE

Bedroom tax

Tracy and her 17-year-old daughter live in a two-bedroom housing association flat. Tracy gets universal credit, which pays her rent of £600 a month in full. Her daughter moves out. Tracy now has a spare bedroom, so her universal credit housing costs element is reduced by 14 per cent of her rent. She now gets universal credit of only £516 a month. Tracy applies for a discretionary housing payment from the local authority, which pays the £84 a month shortfall.

Is there another adult living with you?

The amount you get to help with your rent is reduced if another adult (known as a non-dependant) lives with you whom the government expects to be contributing to the rent – eg, an adult son or daughter. This is the case whether you have a local authority, housing association or private landlord. Some people do not count as non-dependants – eg, your partner, young people included in your benefit claim or joint tenants/lodgers.

For universal credit, £93.02 a month (known as a housing costs contribution) for each non-dependant aged at least 21 is deducted from your housing costs element, even if you do not receive any contribution from that person. However, there are some situations in which no amount is deducted – eg, if you or the non-dependant are getting the daily living component of personal independence payment or adult disability payment (in Scotland), or if the non-dependant has a child aged under five.

Do you pay service charges?
You may be eligible for an amount to help with certain service charges that you have to pay to your landlord as well as rent – eg, some warden/caretaker services or communal lifts.

If you own your home, you may also be eligible for an extra amount in your universal credit or pension credit to help with certain service charges that you have to pay. For universal credit, you cannot get this help until after a waiting period of nine months, or if you are doing any paid work, even if only for a few hours each week.

3. Are you paying a mortgage?

If you are getting universal credit or pension credit and own your own home, you may be able to get a repayable loan to help with mortgage interest payments. For universal credit, you cannot get this help in the first three months of your claim.

The amount of help with your mortgage is not based on what you pay, but is calculated by using a standard interest rate. The money to help with your mortgage is always paid directly to your lender.

You do not need to repay the loan (and the interest on the loan) until the property is sold or transferred to someone else. You should obtain financial advice before taking out the loan.

4. Can you get a discretionary housing payment?

Local authorities have discretion to make extra payments, known as discretionary housing payments, to people finding it difficult to pay rent. To be eligible, you must be entitled to universal credit housing costs element or housing benefit, and must appear to need extra financial help. It is up to the local authority whether or not to pay you, how much and for how long. In Scotland, however, shortfalls due to the bedroom tax and benefit cap should always be met.

5. Can you get help with your council tax?

Council tax is a tax on the home you live in, and is paid to the local authority. In some cases, the home you live in may be exempt from council tax – eg, if everyone over 18 who lives there is a full-time student. In other cases, you may be able to get a discount on your council tax – eg, if you live alone, or are a lone parent and no other adult lives in the property, you can get a discount of 25 per cent.

You may also be eligible for council tax reduction (also called council tax support) from the local authority. You can get this if your income is low enough, and it may help to pay some, or all, of your council tax. In Scotland, water and sewerage costs are billed together with council tax, and these are not met by council tax reduction. Apply to your local authority.

6. Can you get help with heating costs?

In England and Wales, if the temperature in your area is below freezing for seven days in a row, you get a cold weather payment of £25 a week if you are getting universal credit with no earnings and you have a child aged under five or you or your child have a disability. In Scotland, if you meet the same conditions you get a winter heating payment of £59.75, paid regardless of temperature.

In Scotland, you also get a child winter heating payment of £255.80 if your child is entitled to the highest rate of the care component of child disability payment.

If you are over pension age, you get a winter fuel payment or, in Scotland, pension age winter heating payment. If you get pension credit, you can also get the cold weather payment or, in Scotland, winter heating payment.

These payments are made automatically if you qualify, you do not need to apply.

If you are on a low income or receive a qualifying benefit, you may be entitled to help with fuel costs – ie, energy efficiency assistance or reduced energy bills. You should contact the Energy Saving Trust, your local authority or energy provider.

Further information

If you need housing advice, contact the Shelter helpline: 0808 800 4444; Wales: 08000 495 495. You can also find online advice and a webchat service at england.shelter.org.uk/get_help or scotland.shelter.org.uk/get_help or sheltercymru.org.uk/get-help

Find out more about the Energy Saving Trust at energysavingtrust.org.uk

Chapter 7
Disability in the family

This chapter covers:

1. What help is available?
2. Do you have a disabled child?
3. Do you or your partner have a disability?
4. Are you caring for someone who is disabled?
5. Can you get help with transport?
6. How can you reduce your bills?

What you need to know

- If you or your child have a disability, you may be entitled to extra help from the social security system.
- If you care for a child or adult with a disability, you may be entitled to extra help.
- If you have a disability, or care for a person with a disability, it is a good idea to get a benefits check.
- You may get help whether you are in or out of work.
- If you disagree with the result of an assessment of your disability, you often have a right to challenge the decision.
- If you live in Scotland, benefits for disabled people and carers are different.

1. What help is available?

If you, or a member of your family, have a long-term health condition or disability, you (or they) may be entitled to a disability benefit. Getting a disability benefit may mean your other benefit payments increase and may mean you can get help with travel costs and reduced bills. If you care for a disabled adult or child, you may be entitled to payments as a carer.

Box A

Financial help if there is disability in the family: checklist

- disability living allowance for children or, in Scotland, child disability payment
- personal independence payment or, in Scotland, adult disability payment
- attendance allowance or, in Scotland, pension age disability payment
- carer's allowance or, in Scotland, carer support payment
- additional amounts for disabled children, disabled adults and carers in universal credit, pension credit, housing benefit or council tax reduction
- national insurance credits
- Motability scheme
- blue badge parking
- vehicle tax exemption or reduction
- concessionary travel
- NHS travel costs
- council tax discounts and reduction
- TV licence fee concessions
- Christmas bonus
- VAT exemption

Also available in Scotland are:

- carer's allowance supplement
- child winter heating payment
- young carer grant

2. Do you have a disabled child?

You may be entitled to benefits or other support if you have a disabled child. Because all children, particularly babies, need a lot of care, not all children with a disability or health condition qualify. If benefit is refused for a young child, a later claim may be successful.

Disability living allowance or child disability payment

If your child has a disability or long-term health problem, you may be able to claim disability living allowance for them, or child disability payment if you live in Scotland. If you move between Scotland and the rest of the UK, see Box B.

Box B

Child moving between Scotland and the rest of the UK

If your child gets **disability living allowance** and you move to Scotland, you should tell the DWP. At the time of writing, disability living allowance continues for 13 weeks and will be transferred to child disability payment without the need for a new claim. However, these rules may change so that automatic transfer is no longer possible and a new claim for child disability payment in Scotland is required.

If your child gets **child disability payment** and you move out of Scotland to another part of the UK, you should tell Social Security Scotland. Child disability payment ends after 13 weeks and you will need to claim disability living allowance for your child instead.

If a child needs more care or supervision than most children of the same age, they may be able to get the disability living allowance or child disability payment care component. This is paid at one of three rates and can be claimed from the age of three months.

If a child is unable to walk or requires additional supervision when walking outside, they may be able to get the mobility component. This is paid at one of two rates. They must be at least three years old to get the higher rate and at least five to get the lower rate. A child can qualify for one or both components.

EXAMPLE

Disability living allowance for children

Barnaby is 14. He has epilepsy. Despite his medication, he has regular seizures. He requires supervision throughout the day, including when walking outdoors, to ensure he does not injure himself when he has seizures. He is entitled to the care and mobility components of disability living allowance. If he lived in Scotland, Barnaby could get both components of child disability payment.

While your child is under 16, a parent or other main carer is authorised to act as their appointee. This means, for example, that you are responsible for completing the relevant forms and making claims on behalf of your child. When your child is 16, they can be responsible for managing their own disability benefit claims, or you can continue to be their appointee if required.

If your child receives disability living allowance or child disability payment, you are entitled to an additional amount in your universal credit, or pension credit, or this may mean you become entitled to these benefits for the first time. This disabled child addition is payable at a lower or higher rate; the higher rate is payable if your child is entitled to the highest rate of the care component of disability living allowance or child disability payment. The disabled child addition is also included if they are getting personal independence payment or adult disability payment, and the higher rate is payable if they get the enhanced rate for daily living.

The amount can be included from the start date of the award of the disability benefit, even if this takes a long time to be decided.

Tell the office dealing with your benefit as soon as possible that your child is getting disability living allowance or child disability payment, or if they start to get the highest rate of the care component. The disabled child addition is payable even if you do not get a basic amount for the child due to the two child limit. If your child is certified as blind or severely sight impaired, the higher rate of the disabled child addition is payable.

EXAMPLE

Additional amounts

Michaela is a lone parent and gets universal credit. Her five-year-old son has been diagnosed with autism and needs additional care. She applies for disability living allowance for him and gets the care component middle rate. She can now get a disabled child element and a carer element included in her universal credit. She should tell the DWP that her son is now getting disability living allowance. If Michaela lived in Scotland and her child was getting child disability payment, she would get the additional amount in her universal credit.

If your child gets disability living allowance or child disability payment, you are exempt from the benefit cap. Chapter 11 has details of the benefit cap.

What happens when your child is 16?

If you are getting disability living allowance for your child, the DWP may invite them to claim personal independence payment when they turn 16. If this happens, they must claim personal independence payment, otherwise their disability living allowance will end. However, not all children who are entitled to disability living allowance will qualify for personal independence payment, because the rules are different. If your child's personal independence payment claim is turned down, they can challenge that decision.

Your child can remain on disability living allowance after age 16 if:

- they are in hospital; disability living allowance can continue until they leave hospital
- they have a terminal illness
- they live in Scotland; their disability living allowance can continue until they are 18, unless they choose to claim adult disability payment or are transferred to child disability payment before then

Note: If you live in Scotland, you can only make a new claim for child disability payment before your child turns 16, but entitlement can continue until they are 18, or 19 in some cases. They can claim adult disability payment when they reach 16, or wait until they are 18, but you should seek advice as the rules are different and they could end up with less benefit. Your child is usually responsible for managing their own child disability payment or adult disability payment claim when they turn 16, but if they are unable to, you can continue to be their appointee.

When your child turns 16, you may be able to continue to claim child benefit and additional amounts in universal credit or pension credit for them, or they may be able to claim universal credit in their own right if they have a disability, and depending whether they are continuing in education. Get a benefit check to find which option would give your family the most income.

The Family Fund

The Family Fund provides grants to buy specific items to help care for a child under 18 who has a severe disability or a serious illness. You can apply if you get universal credit or pension credit. Even if you do not get one of these, you can still apply but any help you are entitled to depends on your household income. Find out more at familyfund.org.uk.

3. Do you or your partner have a disability?

If you have a disability or long-term health condition, there are benefits you may be able to get. Your entitlement does not depend on how much income or savings you have, and you do not need to have paid national insurance contributions. Which one you claim depends on your age and where you live.

- **Personal independence payment or, in Scotland, adult disability payment:** you can claim this if you are aged 16 or older. There is a mobility component and a daily living component, each paid at a standard or enhanced rate.

- **Attendance allowance or, in Scotland, pension age disability payment:** you can claim this if you have reached pension age. There is a lower rate and a higher rate depending on how much care you need. If you are already getting personal independence payment or adult disability payment, you do not need to switch when you reach pension age; you renew your existing benefit instead.
- **Disability living allowance**, or, in Scotland, **Scottish adult disability living allowance**: you cannot make a new claim as an adult, but in some cases, usually if you are over pension age, you may still be getting it if you were not invited to claim personal independence payment instead. There is a mobility component payable at a lower or higher rate, and a care component payable at a lowest, middle or highest rate.

If you move between Scotland and the rest of the UK, see Box C.

Box C

Adult moving between Scotland and the rest of the UK

If you or your partner get **personal independence payment (or attendance allowance)** and move to Scotland, you should tell the DWP. At the time of writing, payment will continue and you will be transferred to adult disability payment (or pension age disability payment) without having to make a new claim. However, these rules may change so that automatic transfer is no longer possible and a new claim will be required.

If you or your partner get **adult disability payment (or pension age disability payment)** and move out of Scotland to another part of the UK, you should tell Social Security Scotland. Adult disability payment (or pension age disability payment) ends after 13 weeks and you will need to claim personal independence payment (or attendance allowance) instead.

What families say

Personal independence payment

'PIP has afforded me not only physical independence but allows me some financial control through the choice of how to spend the money I receive. My choices will differ from others' as much as our symptoms, circumstances and requirements.' *Lili, Changing Realities*

'Now that I'm getting [PIP] I just feel loads better, honestly. A weight off my shoulders. I can't do a lot of things [but in future] I want to do things, I want to be working, that still is my goal, just in the meantime right now I can't. It's good to have this period of slightly higher income... I feel like I can just breathe right now.' *Young UC claimant, Early Warning System*

EXAMPLES

Benefits for disability

Joshua is 26. He has a mental health condition and is only able to take care of himself with prompting from others. He struggles to interact with people and cannot go out on his own as he has panic attacks. Joshua is entitled to both the daily living and mobility components of personal independence payment.

Ildiko is 67. She has arthritis which particularly affects her legs, hips and hands. She needs help getting dressed, washed and using the toilet. She is entitled to attendance allowance.

You make a claim for personal independence payment by phone. You are then usually asked to complete a 'How your disability affects you' form (a paper or digital version), including details of your care needs and the difficulties you have getting around. You may also be asked to attend an assessment in person, by video or phone.

You make a claim for attendance allowance on a paper form, available online or by phoning the attendance allowance helpline. This form allows you to provide details of your care needs. Some people who claim attendance allowance are asked to attend an assessment in person.

Social Security Scotland administers adult disability payment and pension age disability payment. You start a claim online or by phone. You also need to provide details of how your disability is affecting you, either online or on a paper form. You will only be asked to attend an assessment (a consultation) if it is considered necessary in order to determine entitlement.

What CPAG says

Supporting information

Providing additional information, such as medical reports or supporting statements, can help ensure that the correct decision is made about your benefit entitlement. Although the DWP can request information from your doctor or another professional, it does not always do this so try to get this additional information yourself if possible. Send it to the office dealing with your claim. Make sure any evidence you send supports your application. Supporting statements can come from someone who cares for you, a member of your family or any professionals who work with you or your family. Make a copy of the form and the evidence before you send it.

For adult disability payment you will be asked to provide additional supporting information, but Social Security Scotland will obtain this for you if you ask and give permission for this.

If you go into hospital or a care home, some or all of your disability benefits may end after a period of time. You should tell the DWP, or Social Security Scotland if you get adult disability payment, as soon as you can to avoid having to repay any overpaid benefit.

If you have a terminal illness, you may be automatically entitled to the personal independence payment daily living component or attendance allowance. If you live in Scotland and are terminally ill, you may be entitled to both components of adult disability payment. You still need to make a claim.

If you get disability living allowance, personal independence payment or adult disability payment, you are exempt from the benefit cap. There is more about the benefit cap in Chapter 11.

These disability benefits are not counted as income when assessing your entitlement to means-tested benefits, and can increase the amount of universal credit (if you or your partner are over pension age), pension credit, housing benefit or council tax reduction you get. Contact the office dealing with your other benefits as soon as possible to say that you are getting a disability benefit.

You may also be able to qualify for employment and support allowance, depending on your national insurance contributions. If you get universal credit, you can provide medical evidence and request an assessment of your disability or illness, which may reduce your work-related requirements and increase the amount you get. There is more about this in Chapter 5.

4. Are you caring for someone who is disabled?

You are a carer if you are spending at least 35 hours a week looking after a severely disabled person. The person you look after could be your child, partner, or another relative or friend, but they must be getting one of the following disability benefits:

- the daily living component of personal independence payment or adult disability payment
- the middle or highest rate of the care component of disability living allowance or child disability payment
- attendance allowance or pension age disabilty payment

As a carer, you may be able to get:

- carer's allowance or, in Scotland, carer support payment
- a carer element included in your universal credit or a carer addition in your pension credit

To get **carer's allowance**, you must not earn more than the earnings limit (approximately 16 hours a week at the minimum wage) nor be a full-time student.

To get **carer support payment** in Scotland, you must not earn more than the earnings limit, but you can qualify if you are a full-time student.

Box D

Carer element

If you are entitled to carer's allowance or carer support payment, you get a carer element in your universal credit. Carer's allowance or carer support payment counts as income in full for universal credit, but it is usually worth claiming to make sure you are recognised as a carer.

You can get a carer element in universal credit even if you do not get carer's allowance or carer support payment, including if this is because you earn more than the earnings limit. You must meet the other conditions about providing care of at least 35 hours a week for a severely disabled person.

If you are a full-time student, you can only get a carer element if you are entitled to carer support payment in Scotland.

Report on your online journal or by phone as soon as possible to say that you are caring for a disabled person or entitled to carer's allowance or carer support payment.

If your universal credit includes a carer element, you do not need to look for work or attend any interviews about work (see Chapter 5 for more details). If you get a carer element, you are exempt from the benefit cap (see Chapter 11 for more details).

If you or your partner are entitled to carer's allowance or carer support payment and get pension credit, you get a carer addition. Tell the Pension Service as soon as possible if you are entitled to carer's allowance or carer support payment. This includes if you have claimed carer's allowance or carer support payment but have been told it cannot be paid to you because you receive a state pension or other overlapping benefit. Carer's allowance or carer support payment counts as income in full for pension credit, but you must claim it to get the carer addition in pension credit.

If the person you look after gets pension credit, get advice before claiming carer's allowance, carer support payment or the carer element in universal credit, as your claim may affect their benefit amount and they may be worse off.

Only one person can qualify as a carer for one disabled person, so if you have a disabled child, you and your partner must choose who should claim. If you and your partner each look after different people, you can each qualify and get two carer elements in universal credit.

Getting carer's allowance, carer support payment or caring for someone could mean you become entitled to universal credit or pension credit for the first time.

EXAMPLE

Carer's allowance

Sam and Dave have a disabled child who gets the highest rate of the disability living allowance care component. Both Sam and Dave provide care for more than 35 hours a week. Dave does not work so they decide that he will claim carer's allowance as the main carer. He gets carer's allowance. The couple then get an additional amount (a carer element) in their universal credit.

If you live in Scotland, you are entitled to an additional **carer's allowance supplement** if you are getting carer's allowance or carer support payment on specified dates. This is a lump sum that is paid automatically twice a year. It does not affect other benefits.

In Scotland, young carers aged at least 16 and under 19, who care for a disabled person but are not getting carer support payment, may be eligible for a **young carer grant** of £390.25.

National insurance credits

If you care for someone for at least 20 hours a week, you may be entitled to national insurance credits. These help fill any gaps in your contribution record (eg, because you are not in paid work), and so help to protect your future entitlement to benefits – eg, your state pension. If you receive carer's allowance or carer support payment, you get these credits automatically. If you do not receive carer's allowance, you can claim the credits from the DWP on Form CC1.

5. Can you get help with transport?

Motability

If you get the enhanced rate mobility component of personal independence payment or adult disability payment, or your child gets the higher rate mobility component of disability living allowance or child disability payment, and your (or their) award has at least 12 months left to run, you can get assistance with the cost of buying or hiring a car through the Motability scheme. To apply, contact Motability on 0300 456 4566 or visit motability.co.uk.

Blue badge parking

If you get the mobility component of personal independence payment or adult disability payment, or your child gets the mobility component of disability living allowance or child disability payment, you may be able to get a blue badge from your local authority. This allows you more flexibility in where you can park. Even if you do not get these benefits, you may still be able to get a blue badge if you have a disability which affects your walking or driving. Apply online at gov.uk/apply-blue-badge. If you are refused a blue badge, ask the local authority to reconsider its decision.

Vehicle tax reduction

If you or your child get any of the following benefits, you can get an exemption from vehicle tax for one car registered in the disabled person's name or in the name of a nominated driver, provided it is used by, or for, the disabled person:

- the higher rate mobility component of disability living allowance or child disability payment
- the enhanced rate mobility component of personal independence payment or adult disability payment
- armed forces independence payment
- war pensioners' mobility supplement

If you get the standard rate mobility component of personal independence payment or adult disability payment, you get a 50 per cent discount on vehicle tax. There is no exemption or discount for the lower rate of disability living allowance or child disability payment.

Concessionary travel

If you have difficulty getting about, you may be entitled to a concessionary travel card that allows free or subsidised access to public transport. Local authorities manage concessionary travel schemes. Contact your local authority to find out more.

You may also qualify for a disabled persons railcard. This gives you and a travelling companion one-third off rail fares. For details, see disabledpersons-railcard.co.uk or phone 0345 605 0525.

NHS travel costs

If you or your child are travelling to medical appointments, you may be able to get help with travel costs if your income is low enough. You can find out more at nhs.uk/nhs-services/help-with-health-costs/healthcare-travel-costs-scheme-htcs.

In Scotland, you can also apply to the Young Patients Family Fund for help with travel and food costs while your child is in hospital. You can find out more at mygov.scot/young-patients-family-fund.

Depending on your income, you may be able to get help with other NHS costs, such as sight tests and glasses, wigs and fabric supports. See the 'Health benefits' section in Chapter 12 for more information.

6. How can you reduce your bills?

Council tax

You may be able to reduce your council tax bill in one or more of the following ways.

- You can get a reduction in your council tax if you (or anyone you live with) have a disability and you have space in your home to enable you to use a wheelchair in your home, or you need an extra room, bathroom or kitchen to meet your disability needs.
- Your council tax bill is based on the assumption that two adults live in the property and a discount is given if there is only one. Your bill can be discounted if you (or anyone you live with) are severely mentally impaired – eg, if you have Alzheimer's disease or have had a stroke. You may also be able to get a discount if you are caring for someone (not your partner) in your home – eg, an adult son or daughter or another relative or friend.
- If your income is low, you may get help with your bill from your local authority's council tax reduction scheme: see Chapter 6.

If you have a council tax bill to pay, check whether any of these might apply and make sure the local authority knows that you or someone you live with get a disability or carer's benefit.

Heating costs

If you are getting universal credit and have a disabled child in the family, you could get a cold weather payment of £25 a week during any week of freezing cold weather or, in Scotland, a winter heating payment of £59.75, paid regardless of temperature. You can also qualify if you have limited capability for work and get universal credit, but you must have no earnings.

If you live in Scotland and a child aged 18 or under in your household gets the highest rate care component of child disability payment, or the enhanced rate daily living component of adult disability payment on a set week in September, you can get a child winter heating payment of £255.80. It is paid automatically in November.

TV licence

If you are blind (severely sight impaired), you can apply for a 50 per cent concession on your TV licence fee. The licence must be in the name of the person who is blind. If you live with someone who is blind, the TV licence can be transferred into their name (this includes children). If you, or someone you live with, is over 75 and getting pension credit, a free TV licence is available to cover everyone at your address. For details, see gov.uk/free-discount-tv-licence.

Christmas bonus

If you get one of a number of benefits, including personal independence payment, adult disability payment, disability living allowance, child disability payment, attendance allowance or pension age disability payment, you should get a £10 Christmas bonus (paid automatically). If you do not get the bonus, contact the DWP.

VAT

If you or your child are disabled or have a long-term illness, you are not charged VAT on any products designed or adapted for your own or your child's use, or for their installation or repair. For details of eligibility and how to get the products VAT free, see gov.uk/financial-help-disabled/vat-relief or speak to the supplier.

What CPAG says

Poverty is bad for your health

Living on a low income makes it more likely that you or your child will have a long-term physical or mental illness. Bad housing, damp or cold homes can damage a child's health and their educational achievement. Not everyone knows what financial support is available and it is easy to miss out on help that can make a real difference. If anyone in the family has a disability, or cares for a person with a disability, it is always a good idea to get a benefit check.

Further information

Carers UK has a helpline for carers: 0808 808 7777. It also offers a phone service with pre-recorded information and signposting: 0800 888 6999. See also carersuk.org

Contact has a helpline for families with a disabled child: 0808 808 3555; see also contact.org.uk

Chapter 8
Bereavement in the family

This chapter covers:

1. What help is available?
2. Who should you contact?
3. Has your child died?
4. Has your partner died?
5. Were you caring for the person who has died?
6. Can you get help with the funeral costs?

What you need to know

- If you have a bereavement in the family, this is a change of circumstances that affects your benefit entitlement.
- If any of your benefits include an amount for someone who has now died, these should be reassessed.
- If the person who has died was getting benefits, these must be cancelled.
- You may be entitled to help with the cost of the funeral and may qualify for other benefits.

1. What help is available?

When there is a family bereavement, it can be an emotional and stressful time. You may be worried about money. Get advice if you are unsure what to do about cancelling the deceased's benefits or want to know what help you may now be able to get.

Box A
Financial help for bereavement: checklist
- funeral payments
- bereavement benefits
- impact on other benefits

2. Who should you contact?

You should report the death of a family member to the relevant government departments as soon as you can, to avoid any benefit overpayment. A service that can help with this, called Tell Us Once, is available in England, Scotland and Wales to notify all the relevant government departments. When you register the death with your local authority, the registrar will explain what to do, or see gov.uk/after-a-death/organisations-you-need-to-contact-and-tell-us-once for more information.

3. Has your child died?

If your child has died, entitlement to some benefits continues for a specified number of weeks after the death and other benefits stop from the date of death.

Child benefit continues for eight weeks, then stops.

Universal credit continues to include the child element, any disabled child element, carer element and bedroom allocation, in the assessment period in which the death occurred and the following two monthly assessment periods. Universal credit will still be affected by changes in income – eg, if your earnings have reduced it will go up.

You are not required to look for work or be available for work within six months of the death. In practice, all work-related requirements are 'switched off' for six months, but you may receive a phone call after three months to ask whether you want to attend a work-focused interview. If you do not want to, no action will be taken until the end of the six-month period.

Pension credit child amounts continue for eight weeks after the death, as does carer's allowance or carer support payment.

Disability living allowance, personal independence payment or adult disability payment stop from the date of death.

In Scotland, child disability payment stops, but there is a payment covering eight weeks from the date of death.

Scottish child payment also stops, but there is a payment covering 12 weeks from the date of death.

Healthy Start or Best Start foods stop, but you can still use any remaining credit on your card.

You have the right to two weeks' statutory parental bereavement leave if your child under 18 dies. You may also qualify for statutory parental bereavement pay from your employer. Bereavement support payment is not payable for the death of a child.

If a baby is stillborn after 24 weeks or dies, you are still entitled to a Sure Start maternity grant or Best Start grant pregnancy and baby payment, and do not have to pay it back if you have already received it. You can also get a funeral payment.

If you get universal credit or pension credit, you are entitled to help with funeral costs.

If a benefit continues in payment for longer than it should, it is an overpayment which you can be asked to repay, but there is always discretion not to require you to repay in exceptional circumstances.

4. Has your partner died?

If your partner has died, there will be some changes to your benefit entitlement.

Universal credit continues and you do not need to make a new claim. The amount continues to include the couple rate and any additional amounts for your partner in the assessment period in which they died and for the following two monthly assessment periods. Your partner's income stops and is no longer taken into account.

You are not required to look for work or be available for work within six months of the death. In practice, all work-related requirements are 'switched off' for six months, but you may receive a phone call after three months to ask whether you want to attend a work-focused interview. If you do not want to, no action will be taken until the end of the six-month period.

If you were not getting universal credit before your partner died, you need to claim as soon as you can after the death. Your claim will not be backdated unless you supply medical evidence of illness or you have a disability that meant you were unable to claim up to one month earlier.

Pension credit stops if it was in your partner's name. If you are over pension age, you need to make a new claim for pension credit as a single person, which can be backdated up to three months with no reason required. If you are under pension age, you need to claim universal credit instead. If you are already the claimant for pension credit, the amount is adjusted to a single rate and your partner's income is no longer taken into account.

You need to report changes in income or capital (savings) for universal credit or pension credit.

Personal independence payment, adult disability payment, attendance allowance or pension age disability payment stop from the date of death.

If your partner was claiming child benefit for your child(ren), this must be cancelled with the Child Benefit Office. You can make a new claim in your name, which can be backdated up to three months with no reason required.

If your partner was claiming Scottish child payment for your children, you need to make a new claim in your own name, which cannot be backdated.

If you are under pension age, and your partner paid sufficient national insurance contributions in any one year of their working life, you may be entitled to bereavement support payment. You can qualify if you were married or registered civil partners, or if you were cohabiting and responsible for a child. You are entitled to a lump sum and an ongoing payment for 18 months if you claim within three months of the death. If you claim later than three months after the death, it is payable for a reduced period. If you claim more than 12 months after the death, you do not get the lump-sum payment. Bereavement support payment is payable as well as universal credit, and does not reduce the amount of universal credit you get.

If you get universal credit or pension credit, you are entitled to help with funeral costs.

You may also qualify for council tax single adult discount and a council tax reduction due to your income. Ask your local council about this and other discounts available to you.

If universal credit continues to include an amount for your partner for longer than it should, this is an overpayment which you may be asked to repay, but there is discretion not to require you to repay in exceptional circumstances. If other benefits continue in payment, they may be recovered from your late partner's estate.

5. Were you caring for the person who has died?

If you were caring for the person who has died and getting carer's allowance, or carer support payment in Scotland, you should tell the DWP Carer's Allowance Unit or Social Security Scotland about the death. Your carer's allowance or carer support payment continues for eight weeks from the date of death, then stops.

If you are a carer and have been getting universal credit with a carer element, tell the DWP so your benefit can be reassessed. The carer element is paid for the remainder of the monthly assessment period in which the death occurred and for the next two complete months, then stops. After that, you may be expected to be more active in finding work. See Chapter 5 for more information.

6. Can you get help with the funeral costs?

In England and Wales, if your partner, child, family member or close friend has died, you may qualify for a **funeral expenses payment** to help with the costs of their funeral. In Scotland, you may qualify for a **funeral support payment**. Note that this might not cover the full costs of a funeral, which can be expensive. To qualify, you must be getting a qualifying benefit (see Box B).

Box B

Qualifying benefits for funeral expenses payment and, in Scotland, funeral support payment

- universal credit
- housing benefit
- pension credit
- income-related employment and support allowance

If your partner or child has died, it is accepted that you are responsible for the funeral costs. If another family member or friend has died, you must show it is reasonable for you to accept responsibility for the funeral expenses. This means you may have to show there is no one who was closer to the person who has died and who could be expected to take responsibility, such as their partner, parent, son or daughter. You must also have accepted liability for the costs, not just started making the arrangements.

The person who has died must have been living in the UK when they died. Usually, the funeral must also take place in the UK, although funerals in European Economic Area countries or Switzerland may also qualify in some circumstances.

You can claim at any time from the date of death up to six months after the date of the funeral. If you have claimed one of the qualifying benefits but it has not yet been awarded, the decision on the funeral payment may be delayed until your claim for a qualifying benefit has been decided. Alternatively, you may be refused a funeral payment. If this happens, you can reclaim within three months of being awarded the qualifying benefit, or in Scotland the decision can be redetermined.

If you qualify for a funeral payment, you are entitled to a payment to cover:

- the costs of a burial plot and burial fees (but not the cost of burying ashes following a cremation)
- cremation fees
- the costs of any documentation needed to release any assets
- certain transport costs
- up to a further £1,000 (£1,279.15 in Scotland) for any other funeral expenses – eg, a funeral director's fees, religious costs and flowers

If the person who died had a funeral plan, the amount may be reduced.

In England, you may be entitled to a payment from the children's funeral fund if the funeral is for a child under 18 or a baby stillborn after the 24th week of pregnancy. The funeral must take place in England and you must be responsible for organising it, though the funeral director usually applies for the payment. It covers burial or cremation fees and an amount for a coffin. You can also apply for a funeral expenses payment. You do not have to get a qualifying benefit or have a low income to get a children's funeral fund payment.

Further information

For what to do when someone dies, see gov.uk/after-a-death

For support when a child dies, call Child Bereavement UK's helpline on 0800 028 8840 or see childbereavementuk.org

For anyone affected by pregnancy loss or the death of a baby, call the SANDS helpline on 0808 164 3332, email helpline@sands.org.uk or see sands.org.uk

For any type of pregnancy loss, call Tommy's Midwives' helpline on 0800 0147 800, email midwife@tommys.org or see tommys.org/baby-loss-support

For bereavement support, call the Cruse bereavement support helpline on 0808 808 1677 or see cruse.org.uk

Chapter 9
Children in care

This chapter covers:

1. What help is available?
2. Has your child gone into care?
3. Are you a foster carer?
4. Are you looking after a child under a kinship care arrangement?

What you need to know

- If your child goes into care, your benefit entitlement may change almost immediately.
- If you are a kinship carer, you may be entitled to family benefits for the child you care for.
- Getting good advice as soon as possible is crucial to prevent overpayments and underpayments.

1. What help is available?

If a child is unable to live with their birth family, they may go to live with other family members or friends, or be in the care of the local authority and placed with a foster carer or in a residential establishment. This chapter explains which benefits should be paid in these situations, so you can avoid being underpaid or overpaid.

2. Has your child gone into care?

Some of your benefits may change if your child goes into care – eg, if they go to stay in a residential unit or secure accommodation, or have been placed with foster carers. You may have agreed to this or it may be because of a legal order. Your child may be described as being looked after away from home, looked after and accommodated or in the care of the local authority.

Note: some of the following changes do not apply if your child is in residential accommodation provided *solely* because of their disability or because their health would be significantly impaired if the accommodation were not provided.

- **Child benefit**. This stops after your child has been in care for eight weeks in a row. Tell the Child Benefit Office if your child has been looked after away from home for eight weeks. This is your responsibility, even though the local authority should tell the Child Benefit Office on Form CH193 when a child comes into care.
- **Universal credit.** The child element stops when your child is in care. If you are getting the disabled child element or any childcare costs help for them, these also stop. The amount you are allowed to earn before your universal credit starts being affected (your work allowance) may change. If you are in rented accommodation, the amount included in your universal credit for housing costs is calculated as if the child were still living with you for the first six months of their being in care. Tell the DWP immediately.
- **Pension credit.** The child element, and any disabled child element, stops when your child is in care. Tell the Pensions Service immediately.
- **Housing benefit**. Your child stops counting as part of your household as soon as they are in care, so your housing benefit no longer includes amounts for them. Your benefit may also be reduced if you are considered to need fewer bedrooms, as Chapter 6 shows. Tell your local authority housing benefit office immediately. If you are under pension age, you cannot get

housing benefit unless you are in temporary homeless accommodation or specified supported accommodation.

- **Disability living allowance or, in Scotland, child disability payment.** If your child is living with a foster carer, both the mobility component and the care component continue to be paid. If they are in a residential unit/school, the care component stops after four weeks. Tell the Disability Service Centre (for disability living allowance) or Social Security Scotland (for child disability payment) immediately. If your child's disability living allowance was paid to you as their appointee, the appointeeship stops if they are expected to be in care for more than 12 weeks. The foster carer or local authority may become the appointee instead. Tell the Disability Service Centre. If your child has gone into care, Social Security Scotland may appoint someone else to deal with your child's child disability payment.
- **Carer's allowance or, in Scotland, carer support payment**. Your carer's allowance or carer support payment stops if you are no longer caring for your disabled child for 35 hours or more a week, or because their disability living allowance or, in Scotland, child disability payment care component has stopped. If you are getting universal credit, the carer element stops as soon as you are no longer caring for the child. If you get an amount for being a carer in pension credit, this stops eight weeks after your entitlement to carer's allowance or carer support payment stops. If you are claiming carer's allowance for looking after your child, notify the Carer's Allowance Unit or, for carer support payment, notify Social Security Scotland immediately. If you get universal credit, pension credit or housing benefit, tell the DWP and/or local authority that your carer's allowance has stopped.
- **Scottish child payment.** If the child goes into care, you stop getting Scottish child payment when you stop being responsible for them and/or you stop getting a qualifying benefit. If you get child benefit for the child, this will probably be at the same time as your child benefit stops. Chapter 12 has information about Scottish child payment and when you are responsible for a child.

Does your child come home for some of the time?

There are different rules if your child is in care but comes home for some of the time – eg, at weekends or as part of a planned return.

- **Child benefit**. You can get child benefit for any week when your child comes home for seven consecutive nights, or when they come home for any nights immediately following the first seven, or if they come home on a regular basis for at least two consecutive nights each week. Tell the Child Benefit Office of any nights your child spends at home. If you stopped getting child benefit when they went into care, you should make a new claim.
- **Universal credit.** When your child comes home, your universal credit should be adjusted to include the child element, even if they are still being looked after by the local authority. However, if they are only coming home briefly, your universal credit may not increase because of how assessment periods work. For example, if your child comes home then returns to care within the same assessment period, your universal credit will not be increased. Tell the DWP each time your child comes home.
- **Pension credit.** If you have parental responsibility for the child, your pension credit should be adjusted to include the child amount when they come home, even if they are still looked after by the local authority.
- **Housing benefit**. If your child comes home for part of the week, the local authority can calculate your housing benefit as if they were home for the whole week if it is reasonable to do so, taking into account the nature and frequency of their visits. Tell the housing benefit office of any nights your child spends at home.
- **Disability living allowance or, in Scotland, child disability payment**. If your child's care component in their disability living allowance or child disability payment has stopped because they are in residential care, it can be paid for any days they are at home. The day they come home and the day they go back count as days at home. Tell the Disability Service Centre or, for child disability payment, Social Security Scotland of any days the child spends at home.

- **Carer's allowance or, in Scotland, carer support payment**. If your child is disabled and gets the disability living allowance or child disability payment care component (paid at the middle or highest rate), you may be able to get carer's allowance or carer support payment if they start coming home for some of the time and you are caring for them for 35 hours or more a week (Sunday to Saturday). The hours do not have to be spread across the whole week. You may need to make a new claim. If you are getting any means-tested benefits, or if you think you may be entitled because you are now getting carer's allowance or carer support payment, tell the DWP and/or housing benefit office.
- **Scottish child payment**. If your Scottish child payment for a child has stopped because they are in care, it should start being paid again once you are responsible for them again, providing you satisfy the other entitlement rules. This is likely to be when child benefit becomes payable again.

3. Are you a foster carer?

If you are looking after a child under a formal or public fostering arrangement, you are excluded from claiming most family-related benefits for that child. Instead, you should be receiving a fostering payment from the local authority or the fostering agency which has arranged the foster placement.

- **Child benefit**. You cannot claim child benefit for a child you are fostering.
- **Universal credit**. You cannot include a foster child in your universal credit claim – they do not count as your dependant. This means you do not get a child element or disabled child addition for them, and cannot get any help with your childcare costs for that child included in your universal credit. When the DWP looks at how many bedrooms you are allowed for the housing costs element, a child you are fostering is not included. You are allowed one additional room because you are a foster carer, regardless of how many children you are fostering. None of the payments you get for fostering count as income. If you are

the main foster carer for a child aged under one, you do not have any work-related requirements in your claimant commitment. If the child is over one but under 16, you may be expected to go for work-focused interviews if you are a single foster carer or the main foster carer in a couple. This can be extended beyond the child's 16th birthday if they have additional care needs, and can be extended for the same reason to both members of a couple if both are foster carers.

- **Pension credit**. You cannot get a child amount for a child you are fostering. None of the payments you get for fostering count as income.
- **Housing benefit (if you are over pension age)**. A child you are fostering is not included in your housing benefit award – they do not count as your dependant. If you are living in private rented accommodation, your housing benefit is probably calculated using the local housing allowance. This is based partly on how many bedrooms you are considered to need (the size criteria). The size criteria does not include rooms for foster children. However, you are allowed one extra room in the size criteria because you are a foster carer, regardless of how many children you are fostering. Any fostering payment you get does not count as income.
- **Disability living allowance or, in Scotland, child disability payment**. If the child you care for is entitled to one of these benefits, they can receive it while in foster care and you can be the appointee (and be paid the benefit on the child's behalf).
- **Carer's allowance or, in Scotland, carer support payment**. If the child you care for gets disability living allowance or child disability payment care component paid at the middle or highest rate (or the daily living component of personal independence payment or adult disability payment), you can get carer's allowance or carer support payment provided you satisfy the other conditions of entitlement. You can only get carer's allowance or carer support payment if you are earning below a certain level. Fostering income does not count as earnings for carer's allowance or carer support payment.

- **Scottish child payment.** Foster carers cannot get Scottish child payment for a child they are fostering. This is because they do not count as responsible for the child for the purposes of Scottish child payment, as Chapter 12 explains.

4. Are you looking after a child under a kinship care arrangement?

You may be looking after a child who cannot live with their parents. You may be a relative, family friend or connected to the child in another way. This is often called kinship care (or connected persons care or family and friends care). This may be a formal arrangement made through the courts or, in Scotland, the children's hearing system, or arranged within the family or at the request of social workers.

A child in kinship care may or may not be looked after by the local authority; if you are not sure, ask their social worker, if they have one, or the local authority. If the child is looked after, this affects which benefits you can claim.

Is the child looked after by the local authority?

If the child you are caring for is looked after by the local authority, this affects the benefits you can claim. You are treated in a similar way to a foster carer,. with some exceptions.

- **Child benefit.** If the child you care for is looked after and has been placed with you by the local authority and it is paying you under specific legislation, you cannot get child benefit for them. There are some exceptions to this in Scotland, because local authorities have a choice about which legal powers to use to make payments to kinship carers and some types of payment do not prevent you getting child benefit.

- **Universal credit.** If the child is looked after by the local authority, you get no child element, or disabled child element, in your universal credit, unless you have legal parental rights or responsibilities for them. Because you do not get the child element, you get no help with any childcare costs for that child. If you are a single person, or main carer in a couple, you should be exempt from looking for work until the child is 16 or they no longer count as looked after, whichever comes first. This can continue beyond the child's 16th birthday if they have additional care needs. When the DWP looks at how many bedrooms you are allowed for the housing costs element, a looked after child you are caring for is not included. You are allowed one extra room, regardless of how many looked after children you care for.

EXAMPLE

Housing costs element of universal credit

Karen is aged 50 and single. She cares for her three grandchildren (two girls, aged five and seven, and a boy aged 10). This is a kinship care arrangement; all three children are looked after by the local authority. Karen lives in a three-bedroom housing association house. When her housing costs element is calculated, she is assessed as needing one bedroom for herself and one extra bedroom because she is a kinship carer of a looked after child. Because she is only assessed as needing two bedrooms, the bedroom tax restricts the amount of rent that will be covered by the housing costs element of her universal credit. Karen could claim a discretionary housing payment to cover the shortfall or ask social services or children's services for help.

- **Pension credit.** If the child is looked after by the local authority, you do not get a child element unless you have legal parental rights or responsibilities for them.
- **Housing benefit** (if you are over pension age). The child you are caring for is not treated as part of your household for housing benefit purposes, even though they live with you.
  - If you are living in private rented accommodation, your housing benefit is probably calculated using the local housing allowance. This is based partly on how many bedrooms you are considered to need (the size criteria). The size criteria does

not include a looked after child in kinship care. However, you are allowed one extra room in the size criteria because you are a kinship carer of a looked after child. Even if you are caring for more than one looked after child, you are only allowed one extra room.

- **Disability living allowance or, in Scotland, child disability payment**. If the child you care for gets disability living allowance or child disability payment, you can apply to become the appointee and receive it on behalf of the child. If you believe they should be getting disability living allowance or child disability payment, you can make the claim.
- **Carer's allowance or, in Scotland, carer support payment**. If the child you care for gets disability living allowance or child disability payment care component middle or highest rate, you may be able to claim carer's allowance or carer support payment.
- **Scottish child payment**. You should be able to get this for the child, providing you are on universal credit or pension credit.

Box A

How do local authority payments affect your benefits?

As a kinship carer of a looked after child, you should receive a regular payment from the local authority. This payment should be disregarded for benefits.

What if the child is not looked after by the local authority?

If the child you care for is not looked after, or stops being looked after, by the local authority, you should be able to claim any of the benefits, or increases in benefits, a family would usually get, providing you satisfy the normal rules. This includes child benefit and the child element of universal credit, or pension credit. If one or both of the child's parents has died, you may also qualify for guardian's allowance. If you live in Scotland, it may include Scottish child payment.

There are some issues or problems that may arise because you are claiming benefit as a kinship carer.

Box B

Special rules for universal credit

In some circumstances, you can only get amounts in your universal credit for a maximum of two children: the two-child limit. Chapter 2 explains more.

Some non-looked after children in kinship care are exempt from the two-child limit. You can get amounts included for them if one of the following applies:

- the child is living with you as a result of a child arrangements order under section 8 of the Children Act 1989
- you have been appointed as a special guardian for the child under section 14A of the Children Act 1989
- you are entitled to guardian's allowance for the child
- you have a kinship care order under section 11 of the Children (Scotland) Act 1995
- you have been appointed as a guardian for the child under section 5 of the Children Act 1989 or section 7 of the Children (Scotland) Act 1995
- one of the above bullet points applied to you before the child's 16th birthday and you have continued to be responsible for them since then
- you have taken on the care of the child where it is likely that otherwise they would have been looked after by the local authority

This means that even if you already have two or more dependent children and you start caring for a child (or children) in one of these circumstances, you can get the child element in your universal credit for that child. If you give birth to a child after taking on the care of a child or children in one of these circumstances, the child or children in a kinship care arrangement are disregarded when applying the two-child limit.

You may be affected by the benefit cap: see Chapter 11.

Box C

How do local authority payments affect your benefits?

As a kinship carer of a non-looked after child, you may be receiving a regular payment from the local authority – eg, a special guardianship allowance, child arrangements order allowance (previously called a residence order allowance) or, in Scotland, a kinship care allowance. Generally, all these types of payments are disregarded for benefits.

Does someone else also want to claim benefits for the same child?

The main benefits that you may want to claim to cover the additional costs of looking after a child are child benefit and the child element of universal credit or pension credit. A child can only be included in one person's benefit award.

To get child benefit, you must be responsible for the child. This usually means that the child lives with you. 'Living with' means that the child lives in the same house or residence and has a settled course of daily living there. If there are competing claims for child benefit, the person with whom the child normally lives has priority.

However, if someone else is getting child benefit for the child when you make a claim, the other person usually keeps the child benefit for three weeks after you make your claim – this means you do not usually become entitled to child benefit until three weeks after the week in which you claim.

You should get the child element in universal credit as soon as the child normally lives with you. You do not have to be getting child benefit for them. If a child comes to live with you full time and the arrangement is reasonably settled, it is very likely that the child will be treated as normally living with you. This means that if someone else has been getting universal credit for the child, their payments stop. Similar rules apply for pension credit.

You are treated as responsible for a child for housing benefit purposes if they are normally living with you. This means that they spend more time in your household than in any other. If it is unclear in whose household the child normally lives, or if they spend equal time in more than one household, you are treated as having responsibility if one of the following applies:

- you get child benefit for the child
- no one gets child benefit, but you have claimed it
- no one has claimed child benefit, or more than one person has, but you appear to have most responsibility for the child

If the child has a disability and gets disability living allowance or, in Scotland, child disability payment, you can apply to become their appointee. The appointee receives the disability living allowance or child disability payment on behalf of the child. If you believe that the child should be getting disability living allowance or child disability payment, you can make the claim.

If you are caring for a child with a disability and someone else is also providing care for them, you must agree between yourselves who should claim carer's allowance or carer support payment. If you cannot agree, the DWP or Social Security Scotland decides.

Is there a delay in getting your benefit paid?

If you experience delays in getting your benefits sorted out, you may be able to get some financial help from your children's services or social work department to help you continue to care for the child. It is also possible to get an interim payment or an advance of some benefits, if there is a delay with your claim. There is more about delays and what help may be possible in Chapter 11.

Further information

Fosterline (England) has a helpline: 0800 040 7675; see also fosterline.info

Fostertalk has a UK-wide helpline: 0121 758 5013; see also fostertalk.org

If you are a kinship carer in England or Wales, you can use the Kinship advice line: 0300 123 7015; see also kinship.org.uk

In Scotland, the Kinship Care Advice Service helpline is: 0808 800 0006; see also kinship.scot

Chapter 10
Leaving domestic abuse

This chapter covers:

1. What help is available?
2. Can you get universal credit?
3. What help can you get for your children?
4. Can you get help with housing costs?
5. Has domestic abuse affected your health?
6. What help is there if you are from abroad?
7. What can be done about unwanted payments of perpetrators' benefits?
8. What other help is there?

What you need to know

- You may be able to claim universal credit as a single person or, if you are still in a relationship with the perpetrator, make alternative payment arrangements.
- You may be able to get help with your rent through universal credit or housing benefit, and help for your children.
- There are exemptions to the two-child limit for a child likely to have been conceived as a result of rape or in a coercive or controlling relationship.
- If domestic abuse has affected your physical or mental health, you may be able to receive other benefits.
- You may be entitled to claim benefits if you are from abroad.
- Getting good advice as soon as possible is crucial to getting what you are entitled to, as well as protecting yourself.

1. What help is available?

There are special social security rules to help you if you have experienced domestic abuse.

What the law says

What is domestic abuse?

Any incident, or pattern of incidents, of abusive behaviour between those aged 16 or over who are, or have been, intimate partners or family members regardless of gender or sexuality. Behaviour is abusive if it consists of any of the following:

- physical or sexual abuse
- violent or threatening behaviour
- controlling or coercive behaviour
- economic or financial abuse
- psychological, emotional or other abuse

Section 1 Domestic Abuse Act 2021

The benefits you are entitled to depend on your circumstances. Box A lists some of the most common benefits claimed by people leaving an abusive relationship. You may already be getting one of these and will need to update your claim if you have a joint claim with your former partner. In most cases, the rules are the same as for all claims, but there are some exceptions.

Box A

Financial help after leaving an abusive relationship

- universal credit
- child benefit
- housing benefit
- pension credit
- local welfare assistance

Getting advice about the help you are entitled to is important. You can make an appointment with an adviser at Citizens Advice, at a specialist domestic abuse charity such as Solace or Refuge, or with a work coach at the DWP. If you are staying at a refuge, there may be an adviser there who can help you. You can ask for your appointment to be in private.

Do you need to provide evidence about the abuse?

If you are asked to provide evidence of the abuse, you can supply written evidence from a person acting in an official capacity, such as a healthcare professional, social worker, police officer, your employer or a domestic abuse caseworker assigned to you by a charity. If you have been in direct contact with a voluntary group or charity about the abuse, it can provide written evidence for you.

The evidence must show that your circumstances are consistent with those of someone who has had domestic abuse threatened or inflicted during the previous six months. You need to have contacted the person acting in an official capacity and told them about the abuse. You usually need to give the DWP the evidence within one month of making a claim.

2. Can you get universal credit?

If you have left an abusive relationship, you can get universal credit depending on your circumstances and income.

If you were getting universal credit as part of a couple before leaving the relationship, you should report a change of circumstances on your online journal to notify the DWP that you are no longer together, as well as declaring a change of address and any other household changes. You will be paid as a single person for the whole of the assessment period in which you left your partner, and your claim will continue to run on the same monthly assessment period.

If you did not previously get universal credit, you can make a new claim as a single person.

If you have ended your relationship, but are still living in the same property as your ex-partner, you may be able to claim universal credit as a single person. You will need to provide information and evidence to show you are no longer living as a couple. If you are married, you will need to show that you are living as separate households under the same roof.

You may be able to get a universal credit advance while you are waiting for your first payment of universal credit, to enable you to cover essential expenses. You may also be able to get a budgeting advance to help with extra costs such as essential furniture or household equipment. See Chapter 11 for more information.

What families say

Change of circumstances

'[W]ork agreed to reduce my hours whilst I am healing to go to trauma counselling. Universal Credit asked me about change circumstances and health and need a GP Appointment to get a "Fit Note" to evidence the reasonable adjustments at work... Feeling low and emotional exhausted as trying to heal from Domestic abuse trauma but having to jump hoops and feel stigma for reducing hours with work. Worried about such tight budget.' *Artie P, Changing Realities*

What happens if universal credit is paid to your partner?

If your universal credit is usually paid to your partner, and you still live with them, you can ask the DWP to split the monthly payments between you both, or pay them all to you. The DWP must decide that this is in your, or your child's, interest. These alternative payment arrangements are supposed to avoid hardship.

If universal credit was being paid into your former partner's bank account, it is vital that you give the DWP your own account details for your single claim before your first payment is due. Ask the DWP for help if you have difficulties opening an account.

Box B

Two-child limit rules for universal credit

In some circumstances, you can only get amounts in your universal credit for a maximum of two children. This is known as the two-child limit. There is more about this in Chapter 2.

There are exceptions to the two-child limit for a child likely to have been conceived as a result of rape or in a coercive or controlling relationship. You must not be living at the same address as the alleged perpetrator when the exception applies. A controlling or coercive relationship includes behaviour that makes you fear on at least two occasions that violence will be used against you, or causes you serious alarm or distress which has a substantial adverse effect on your day-to-day activities.

You must provide evidence from an approved person that you had contact with them or another approved person about the rape or coercive or controlling relationship. Approved persons include healthcare professionals, social workers and approved organisations such as specialist rape charities. Third-party evidence is not required if there has been a conviction for rape or coercive controlling behaviour in the UK, or a similar offence abroad, or a Criminal Injuries Compensation Scheme award in respect of a sexual offence, physical abuse or mental injury, and it is likely the offence or injury resulted in the conception.

The exception applies to a younger child who is likely to have been conceived as a result of rape or in a coercive or controlling relationship if you have two or more older children. However, it does not apply if it is an older child (or children) who was conceived as a result of rape or in a coercive or controlling relationship, and you then have a third or subsequent child from another, consensual, relationship. This rule about the order of children is subject to an ongoing legal challenge involving CPAG, so get advice if you are in this situation.

At the time of writing, the UK government is under increasing pressure to scrap the two-child limit, and the Scottish government is planning to introduce a new payment for people affected by it.

Do you need to look for work?

The work-related requirements mean that most universal credit claimants need to look for work or face having a sanction applied. Even if you would normally have to meet some (or all) of the work-related requirements, you do not have to do so for 26 weeks (or 13 weeks if you do not have children) if you have recently experienced domestic abuse and you no longer live with the perpetrator.

If you are the main carer of a child, you may be required to take part in work-focused interviews or take steps to prepare for work after the initial 13 weeks. However, DWP guidance suggests any such engagement should be voluntary until the end of the 26-week period.

You can only be exempted from your work-related requirements once in any one-year period under this rule.

If your children have been affected by experiencing or witnessing domestic abuse, you can have a further break in your work-related requirements of up to one month every six months for a period of two years following the abuse.

Can universal credit help with your rent?

Section 4 of this chapter sets out how universal credit can help pay your rent.

If you are in a refuge or temporary homeless accommodation, help with your rent comes from housing benefit, not universal credit.

Are you over pension age?

If you are over pension age, you can claim pension credit as a single person instead of universal credit. You are allowed more to live on and are not required to look for work, and cannot be sanctioned. If you have children, a child addition can be included in your pension credit. You need to claim housing benefit if you have rent to pay. There is more information about this in Chapter 12.

Is your universal credit claim affected by your ex-partner's income or joint property or savings?

Your universal credit claim is not affected by your former partner's income. Any payment of child maintenance is ignored. If you receive spousal maintenance, that counts as your income and does affect your entitlement.

If you have left a property of which you were the owner or joint owner, the value of the property is ignored for at least six months following a relationship breakdown, and for another six months or longer in other circumstances – eg, if you are taking legal advice to return to the property or are taking steps to sell your share.

If you had a joint bank account with your former partner, you will need to open an individual account in your own name to receive payments of benefits. You may be treated as having a 50 per cent share of jointly held savings, but if you cannot access a joint account due to domestic abuse, you should argue with the DWP that the value of the savings is nil as you do not have access to them.

Does the benefit cap affect you?

The total amount of benefit you can be paid may be limited by a benefit cap. There is more about this in Chapter 11.

What CPAG says

Benefit cap grace period

The grace period can provide protection from the benefit cap for some people leaving domestic abuse. If there was a 12-month period when you lived as a couple with your former partner and you met the work/earnings conditions, then the grace period will apply to you, even if you are now separated. The benefit cap should not apply to you for nine months. It is important to seek advice if you think this may apply to you, because the DWP is unlikely to pick this up.

3. What help can you get for your children?

Child benefit

Child benefit is usually paid to the person responsible for a child or young person. If you were not the child benefit claimant before leaving domestic abuse, you should make a new claim if you are the primary carer of the children. There is information about making a claim in Chapter 12. If your former partner argues they should continue receiving child benefit, HM Revenue and Customs has to decide who to pay based on the circumstances, so be sure to disclose the domestic abuse and other relevant details. If you did not get child benefit before because your partner's income was more than £60,000 and you now no longer live with that person, you can ask HM Revenue and Customs to reinstate payment of child benefit or make a new claim yourself.

Box C

Other help for your children

- Are you getting child maintenance from your ex-partner? See Chapter 3 for how to apply. If you have experienced domestic abuse, tell the Child Maintenance Service and it should explain how to make a payment agreement that will keep you safe.
- Check with your local authority or your child's school whether your children can get free school lunches or any other help.
- Do you need help to pay childcare costs? There is information about this in Chapter 4.
- If you live in Scotland and have a child under 16, check whether you can claim Scottish child payment. If that was previously paid to your ex-partner, contact Social Security Scotland and ask for it to be paid to you instead (provided you meet the qualifying conditions).
- If you are pregnant or have a young child and are getting universal credit, you might get help from Healthy Start or Best Start foods, which provide free vitamins and a payment card for milk and vegetables.

4. Can you get help with housing costs?

Universal credit

Universal credit can include an amount for certain costs, called the housing costs element, which can cover your rent and some service charges. It usually only covers the housing costs for the home you live in. However, in certain situations, it can be paid for a home you are not living in.

If you have left your home due to a reasonable fear of violence at your property but intend to return home, the housing costs element can be paid in your absence for up to 12 months. If you have moved into alternative accommodation, you can receive the housing costs element on both properties for up to 12 months as long as you intend to return to your main home.

Sometimes, you cannot get a housing costs element – eg, if you are paying rent to a close relative and you are also living with them.

What CPAG says

Untidy tenancy

If you stay on in the family home and the abuser has moved out, the DWP may say you have an untidy tenancy where their name is on the tenancy. That means the DWP may only pay you half of the rent. This is wrong. Get immediate advice before rent arrears build up. You are entitled to have the full rent included in your universal credit if it is reasonable that you pay it and unreasonable to expect you to move.

Housing benefit

If you are staying in a refuge or emergency temporary accommodation, you may be able to claim housing benefit even though you claim universal credit for yourself and your children. The refuge staff should be able to help you make a claim. There is more about housing benefit in Chapter 6.

If your previous home is rented and you intend to return to it when it is safe to do so, you can get housing benefit for your rent for up to 52 weeks on both homes if you are in fear of domestic abuse in your main home or in fear of violence from an ex-partner with whom you no longer live. If you do not intend to return to your old home, you can get housing benefit on both homes for four weeks.

EXAMPLE

Housing costs paid for both homes

Billie lives in a council property and gets universal credit, including a housing element for her rent. She leaves the property due to domestic abuse and is placed in a refuge. She claims housing benefit for the refuge accommodation and informs the DWP about her situation, stating that she intends to return to her property when it is safe. Billie's housing costs should be paid in her universal credit for up to 12 months, unless her intention to return ends.

Discretionary housing payments

You may be able to get discretionary housing payments if your universal credit or housing benefit does not cover your housing costs in full. The local authority has discretion whether or not to pay you, how much to pay you and over what period. Check your local authority's website for details.

5. Has domestic abuse affected your health?

If the domestic abuse you have experienced has affected your physical or mental health, you may be able to receive other benefits.

If one or more health conditions affect your ability to work, you should declare this when making your universal credit claim, or report your health condition using your online journal if you have an existing claim. You will need to supply medical certificates from your doctor to cover the period of your ill health. You should then be put through the work capability assessment procedure. This may lead to a reduction or removal of work-related requirements. If you have a severe health condition, you may get an additional element in your universal credit.

If you have a long-term health condition that affects your mobility, or that means you need help with daily activities, you may be entitled to personal independence payment or, in Scotland, adult disability payment. If you have reached pension age and need someone to help look after you, you may qualify for attendance allowance or, in Scotland, pension age disability payment instead. See Chapter 12 for more details.

6. What help is there if you are from abroad?

If you are from the European Economic Area and have protection under the Withdrawal Agreement, you may have settled status, which gives you a full right to reside and the same access to benefits as British citizens. If you have pre-settled status, you will need to prove another right to reside to be eligible for means-tested benefits, or may qualify if you are at risk of destitution.

If you are the spouse of a European Economic Area national who has worker status, you will have a right to reside even if you are separated. If you are the primary carer of children in education, whose parent is or has been a European Economic Area worker in the UK, you may have a right to reside in this way.

If you are from outside the European Economic Area and entered the UK as the partner of a European Economic Area national and have left domestic abuse, you may also be able to obtain rights to claim benefits under European law.

If you are from the European Economic Area and do not have protection under the Withdrawal Agreement, or if you are from outside the European Economic Area, you may be excluded from benefits. This is referred to as having no recourse to public funds and means you cannot get universal credit, pension credit, child benefit and disability benefits. If you have been working in the UK, you may be able to get statutory maternity pay or other statutory payments from your employer, or maternity allowance or contributory benefits, as these are not listed as public funds.

Migrant victims of domestic abuse concession

If you are from abroad and entered the UK as the partner of a British citizen or settled person, you may be entitled to claim benefits under a migrant victims of domestic abuse concession when you leave an abusive relationship. If you have no recourse to public funds as a condition of your stay in the UK, the migrant victims of domestic abuse concession allows you access to public funds so that your welfare is not at risk. You can apply for this concession from the Home Office. It allows you limited access to benefits for three months while you apply for indefinite leave to remain in the UK. You should seek specialist immigration advice if you are in this situation.

7. What can be done about unwanted payments of perpetrators' benefits?

Some people who have left an abusive relationship find that they continue to have the perpetrator's benefits paid into their bank account. This can be used as a tool to maintain contact and to perpetuate abusive behaviour. It can be difficult to get these unwanted payments into your account stopped because banks cannot stop incoming payments to an account and the DWP may refuse to discuss the abuser's claim with you, citing data protection rules. You may feel that your only option is to close your bank account and open a new one, which is an unfair administrative burden on you.

This problem has been reported to CPAG in relation to payments of universal credit, personal independence payment and employment and support allowance, but it may be a problem with other benefits too. If unwanted payments of benefit are being made into your bank account in this way, get further advice. If your adviser is unable to resolve the problem, ask them to contact CPAG's judicial review project (see cpag.org.uk/jr for details) for help to resolve the issue.

8. What other help is there?

You may be able to get support from your local authority under its local welfare assistance scheme. This may be useful to help with the costs of setting up a new home. In England, some local authorities run their own local welfare assistance schemes. In Wales and Scotland, the Discretionary Assistance Fund for Wales and the Scottish Welfare Fund are administered by your local authority. Applications are usually online and you can apply for emergency living expenses, the costs of any travel involved in leaving domestic abuse, and essential household items. See Chapter 11 for how to apply.

Your local authority's social work or children's services department can provide cash help in exceptional circumstances if you have children.

You may qualify for council tax reduction if your low income means you cannot afford to pay your council tax. Ask your local council about this and other discounts available to you.

EXAMPLE

Help to ease exceptional pressure on your family

Anita is a lone parent with three children. She has been rehoused following domestic abuse, and needs beds for the children, a cooker and a sofa. She applies to the local welfare assistance scheme and gets a grant to buy these items.

Further information

Freephone 24-hour National Domestic Abuse Helpline: 0808 2000 247; or use online chat at nationaldahelpline.org.uk/chat-to-us-online

Charities like Refuge (refuge.org.uk) and Solace (solacewomensaid.org) support all victims of domestic abuse. They can help you find a refuge vacancy for you and your children, and support you to find local assistance.

Chapter 11
Dealing with problems

This chapter covers:

1. What help is available?
2. Are you waiting for your benefit?
3. Has your benefit been reduced by the benefit cap?
4. Has your universal credit reduced because of how your wages are paid?
5. Has your benefit been reduced by a sanction?
6. Do you disagree with a decision?
7. Have you been overpaid?
8. What other help is there in an emergency?

What you need to know

- You may be able to get a benefit advance while you are waiting for your benefit to be paid.
- If your benefit is reduced because of the benefit cap, you may be eligible for a discretionary housing payment.
- Your universal credit may be reduced depending on when your wages are paid.
- Most decisions, including the decision to sanction your benefit, can be challenged.
- If you are overpaid, you may be able to challenge the decision, or ask for the overpayment to be written off or reduced.
- In an emergency, you may be able to get a local welfare payment, or help from food banks or the local authority.

1. What help is available?

In the benefits system, things often cause hardship or go wrong. When that happens, there are various solutions, depending on what has happened. This chapter describes common situations where people find themselves without money, or are otherwise unhappy with their benefit claim, and potential ways to address these issues.

Box A

Financial help in an emergency: checklist

- short-term benefit advance
- discretionary housing payments
- hardship payments
- compensation payments
- local welfare assistance
- Children Act payments
- food banks and charities

2. Are you waiting for your benefit?

If you are waiting for a decision on your universal credit or waiting for your first payment, you may be able to get a universal credit advance. On request, you can get up to 100 per cent of your estimated award paid within five days; it is often paid more quickly.

To get an advance, you must be in financial need. This means there is a risk to the health and safety of you, your partner or your child(ren) if you are not paid an advance. You must repay the advance out of your universal credit award, which can mean a reduction in your payments for up to 24 months, but you are not charged interest on the advance.

You can also get a universal credit advance at other times – eg, if you are waiting for an increased payment because your circumstances have changed.

For other expenses, you may be able to get a universal credit budgeting advance. You can get a budgeting advance straight away if it is related to employment – eg, childcare, clothing or travel costs. If it is for other costs such as household furniture, you must have been getting universal credit for at least six months. This is a discretionary payment, up to a maximum of £812, which has to be paid back from your future payments of universal credit.

You can get a short-term advance for jobseeker's allowance and employment and support allowance and some other benefits. For child benefit, you can apply for an interim payment.

The DWP encourages you to apply for a universal credit advance using your online account. You can also apply at your initial interview or by phoning the universal credit helpline on 0800 328 5644. For other benefits, you can ask for a short-term advance at the job centre or use the phone number for the specific benefit at gov.uk/short-term-benefit-advance.

3. Has your benefit been reduced by the benefit cap?

The total amount of benefit you can be paid may be limited by a benefit cap. If you are affected, the amount of your housing benefit or universal credit is reduced.

If you have a child and are getting universal credit, the benefit cap is £1,835 a month, or £2,110.85 a month if you live in Greater London. The cap is calculated by totalling all the benefits you receive. Some benefits are excluded – eg, bereavement support payment.

In some situations, you are exempt from the cap, including if:

- you, your partner or any of your children get disability living allowance, personal independence payment or, in Scotland, adult disability payment or child disability payment
- you or your partner get carer's allowance or, in Scotland, carer support payment
- you or your partner are working and your earnings are over a certain amount

If you have been working and earning over a certain amount over the last year, your universal credit will not be reduced by the benefit cap for nine months after you stop work. To make sure this grace period is applied to your universal credit, have details ready of your earnings for the last year when you claim.

If the benefit cap affects you, you should apply for a discretionary housing payment. In Scotland, local authorities are committed to paying discretionary housing payments due to the benefit cap, but in other areas it may be a reduced amount, time-limited or refused altogether. See more information in Chapter 6.

EXAMPLE

The benefit cap

Jamie and Rebecca have three children, all born before 6 April 2017, so they are not affected by the two-child limit. They live outside Greater London and their rent is £700 a month. Their monthly income from benefits would be universal credit of £2,252.72 and child benefit of £262.38. This is a total of £2,515.10 a month. The benefit cap means they can only get a maximum of £1,835 a month from benefits. So their universal credit is reduced by £680.10 a month. They apply to their local authority for a discretionary housing payment to help with their rent.

What families say

Benefit cap

'A client had to leave her full-time job due to her health. While she waits for her PIP and UC health element decisions, she is subject to the benefit cap. After paying her basic bills, she is living off £50 a week for a family of 4.' *Welfare rights adviser, Early Warning System*

'I've just [seen]... this year's council rent and service charge uprates. I expect it to only go up a £1 or so (combined) but it's gone up by over £4 per week. That's over £200 extra in rent per year, which cos of housing benefit caps will be managed by me paying the difference.' *Victoria S, Changing Realities*

4. Has your universal credit reduced because of how your wages are paid?

Universal credit is calculated over a monthly assessment period. Sometimes, two or more sets of pay are taken into account in one assessment period. This can reduce the amount of universal credit you are paid or even end your award. If you are paid per calendar month and your monthly wages are paid early (eg, your normal payday falls on a non-banking day), you may be paid twice in one assessment period and not paid at all in the next. This generally affects people who are paid near the end of their assessment period. If this happens, as soon as you get your universal credit statement showing two sets of wages, ask the DWP to reallocate one set to another assessment period. This only applies if you are paid monthly.

If you are paid four-weekly, you are paid 13 times in a year, meaning there is one assessment period each year in which you are paid twice. If you are paid fortnightly or weekly, your universal credit will also fluctuate throughout the year because of how you are paid.

EXAMPLE

Universal credit and earning patterns

Torin's wages are paid four-weekly. He usually gets a monthly universal credit payment of £300. In his February assessment period he receives two sets of wages, meaning his earnings in this period are too high for him to get any universal credit. The award ends and Torin gets no universal credit for February. His claim is kept open and he is paid his normal payment of £300 next month. Because Torin becomes entitled again within six months, he keeps his universal credit assessment period and payment day.

Your wages cannot be reallocated to another assessment period if you are paid four-weekly, fortnightly or weekly. If your universal credit stops because your wages are too high, your claim is usually kept open so that you can become entitled again without needing to make a new claim within six months, and your assessment period and payment day will stay the same. You should continue to log into your universal credit account and check this happens, or call the universal credit helpline to report that your wages have gone down.

5. Has your benefit been reduced by a sanction?

If you do not fulfil your work-related responsibilities, you may have a sanction applied to your universal credit, jobseeker's allowance or employment and support allowance. This means your benefit is paid at a reduced rate, perhaps even reduced to nil. This can happen if, for example, you do not go to a work-focused interview or if you are found not to be actively looking for work. The sanctions can be severe, so you should always try to avoid one.

What should you do?

A sanction should not be applied if you have a good reason for your actions. All your circumstances should be taken into account when deciding this – including if you were ill, or if your disability, caring responsibilities, language or transport problems meant you could not attend an interview or undertake an activity.

If you are given a sanction, you can challenge the decision, first by asking for a mandatory reconsideration of the decision and then by appealing to an independent tribunal.

EXAMPLE

Challenging a sanction: good reason

Shivani is a lone parent with a child aged two. She gets universal credit. She is told she must go to a skills assessment course, but that day her child is ill and she cannot go. Shivani tells the DWP, but the following week her universal credit is reduced due to a sanction. She asks the DWP to reconsider the decision. She explains her good reason for not attending, including evidence of a doctor's visit with her child. The decision is overturned. Shivani's universal credit is paid in full from when it was reduced.

If your universal credit is sanctioned, you may be able to apply for a hardship payment. These are not made automatically; you must apply. You must have met all your work-related requirements in the week before you apply and the DWP must accept that you cannot meet your basic needs for rent, heating, food and hygiene. You should try to get help from other sources such as family and friends first, but you are not expected to get into credit card or bank loan debt. Hardship payments cover one assessment period; you will need to reapply each month. The best way to make sure you receive a hardship payment is to reapply every universal credit payday that your usual payment is reduced. They are repaid from your universal credit award. You apply by phoning the universal credit helpline on 0800 328 5644.

If your jobseeker's allowance is sanctioned, you can apply for a universal credit hardship payment.

What CPAG says

Challenging a sanction

- Should the requirement have been applied to you in the first place? Does your claimant commitment record that, in fact, you were able to limit your activity in the way you did?
- Were you properly informed of the requirement and what would happen if you failed to comply with it? If not, the sanction may not be lawful.
- Did you, in fact, fail to carry out the requirement? If you turned up for an appointment just a few minutes late, you may be able to argue that this does not mean you failed to comply. If you have to look for work, did you carry out all such activity as could reasonably be expected of you?
- Did you have a good reason for your actions? Good reason is not defined in the law. All the circumstances should be taken into account, including your health, a domestic emergency, transport difficulties, domestic abuse, language/literacy issues, and sincerely held religious or conscientious objections.

6. Do you disagree with a decision?

Can you appeal?

If you disagree with a decision about your benefit, you may be able to challenge it. You can challenge most decisions about benefits by appealing to an independent tribunal.

Before you can appeal, you must ask for the decision to be looked at again (except for housing benefit), called a mandatory reconsideration. If you want to challenge a housing benefit decision, you can appeal without asking for a mandatory reconsideration.

You must usually ask for a mandatory reconsideration within one month of the date the decision was sent to you. If it has been longer than a month, you can still get a decision looked at again if there are special reasons to extend the time limit (for up to one year maximum). You may also be able to get the decision looked at again if there are particular grounds for doing so – eg, if the person making the decision made a mistake. If you are late asking for a mandatory reconsideration, and it is not accepted that the time limit should be extended, you can still appeal, provided it is within 13 months of the original decision.

If you are still unhappy with the decision following a mandatory reconsideration, you can appeal to an independent tribunal. You must do so within one month of the date of the mandatory reconsideration decision. This time limit can be extended by one year from the usual time limit, if there are special reasons for doing so.

You must appeal in writing, preferably using the appropriate appeal form. For housing benefit, use the form provided by your local authority. For child benefit, use Form SSCS5. For other benefits, use Form SSCS1 ('Appeal a social security benefits decision'), which is available from gov.uk/government/collections/court-and-tribunal-forms or apply online at gov.uk/appeal-benefit-decision/submit-appeal.

In Scotland, adult disability payment, child disability payment, pension age disability payment, Best Start grant, funeral support payment, carer support payment, young carer grant and Scottish child payment are administered by Social Security Scotland. If you disagree with a decision (called a determination) about these benefits, you can request a redetermination. To do this, complete the form sent with the determination or call the helpline on 0800 182 2222. You must usually request a redetermination within 31 days of the date you were notified of the determination (within 42 days for adult disability payment and child disability payment). This can be extended by a year if you have a good reason for not requesting it sooner. If you disagree with the redetermination, you can appeal to an independent tribunal.

EXAMPLE

Appealing

Marcel splits up with his partner and moves into his mother's house with his two children. He claims universal credit as a single parent. His claim is refused because the DWP thinks Marcel still lives with his partner. He requests a mandatory reconsideration of the decision, but the decision is not changed. He then appeals to an independent tribunal. The tribunal accepts that Marcel is single and he is awarded universal credit from the date he first claimed it.

Can you complain?

If you are unhappy with the way your claim has been handled, or you experience delays in getting your benefit decided, you could use the DWP, HM Revenue and Customs or local authority complaints procedure. In the first instance, you should take up the issue with the office dealing with it. Contact details should be on any letters you have about your claim. You should follow the relevant complaints procedure.

Once you have gone through all the steps in the complaints procedure, if you are still unhappy with the response, you can take your case to the Independent Case Examiner (DWP benefits), Adjudicator's Office (child benefit) or the Local Government and Social Care Ombudsman (for local authorities).

If you are still not happy, you can contact your MP about the matter and ask them to refer your complaint to the Parliamentary and Health Service Ombudsman.

You can ask for compensation if you are dissatisfied with the way your claim has been administered. You may be able to get compensation from the DWP, HM Revenue and Customs or the local authority if you can show that you have lost out or suffered through their error or delay.

In Scotland, if you want to complain about the way you have been treated by Social Security Scotland, you can call its helpline on 0800 182 2222. If you are still unhappy after it has dealt with your complaint, you can contact the Scottish Public Services Ombudsman.

7. Have you been overpaid?

If more benefit is paid to you than you are entitled to, you have been overpaid.

There are many reasons why benefits are overpaid – eg, if you gave the wrong information when you claimed, you are late reporting a change in your circumstances, or the relevant department does not act on the information you give.

If you are overpaid, you may be asked to repay the overpayment. You should check your award carefully. If you disagree that you have been overpaid or with the amount you have been overpaid, you can challenge the decision.

If you have been overpaid universal credit, jobseeker's allowance or employment and support allowance, you will usually have to repay, even if it was not your fault. The DWP may write off recovery of these overpayments at its discretion, but only does so in exceptional circumstances. For other benefits, even if you agree that you have been overpaid, you may be able to challenge the decision. You only have to repay an overpayment of some benefits if it was caused by your giving incorrect information, or because you failed to tell the benefit authorities of a relevant change in your circumstances. Housing benefit and benefits paid by Social Security Scotland have slightly different rules, and you may have to repay an overpayment even if you gave correct information, if you could have realised you were being overpaid.

Even if you are asked to repay an overpayment, you can ask for some or all of the overpayment to be written off. However, this is at the authority's discretion.

8. What other help is there in an emergency?

Can you get a local welfare payment?

You may be able to get help from your local authority's local welfare assistance scheme. In England, each local authority has its own scheme. In Wales and Scotland, the Discretionary Assistance Fund for Wales and the Scottish Welfare Fund are local authority administered.

You may be able to get help:

- with an immediate short-term need in a crisis – eg, you have insufficient resources, or need help with expenses in an emergency or due to a disaster (eg, a fire in your home)
- to establish yourself in the community following a stay in institutional or residential accommodation, or to help you remain in the community
- to set up a home in the community as part of a planned resettlement programme
- to ease exceptional pressure on your family
- to enable you to care for a prisoner or young offender on temporary release
- with certain travel expenses – eg, to visit someone in hospital, to attend a funeral, to ease a domestic crisis, to visit a child living with their other parent or to move to suitable accommodation

In England, the local scheme is entirely at your local authority's discretion; contact it for details of the help available and how to apply.

In Wales, the Discretionary Assistance Fund for Wales offers non-repayable emergency assistance payments and individual assistance payments. Find out how to apply at gov.wales/discretionary-assistance-fund-daf/how-apply.

In Scotland, the Scottish Welfare Fund provides community care grants and crisis grants. The basic rules for the scheme are set by the Scottish government, with each local authority having some discretion. You should apply to your local authority.

Can you get any other help from your local authority?

In England and Wales, local authorities have a duty under section 17 of the Children Act 1989 to provide services to children in need.

In Scotland, the local authority social work department has powers under section 22 of the Children (Scotland) Act 1995 and section 12 of the Social Work (Scotland) Act 1968 to assist people in need.

In all these cases, assistance can be given in cash or in kind – eg, vouchers to buy food. However, your local authority may refer you to a local food bank rather than providing you with any direct help.

Can you use a food bank?

You may be able to get help from a food bank if there is one in your area. Food banks can provide essential food and household items free of charge to people in need. Some food banks operate under the umbrella organisation called Trussell; others are independent. Food banks are often run from local churches or community centres. You may have to be referred to the food bank by an agency, such as a social worker, GP practice or Citizens Advice.

Can you get help from a charity?

You may be able to get some assistance from a charity, although this may be more likely to help with specific items (eg, furniture) than provide immediate financial help. Which charity to approach can depend on your personal circumstances, such as having a particular health problem or having worked in a particular job.

Further information

See CPAG's *Welfare Benefits Handbook* for more detailed information on benefits

You can find your nearest Trussell food bank at trussell.org.uk

Search for charitable grants at grants-search.turn2us.org.uk

Chapter 12
A to Z of benefits

Note: benefit rates and some earnings rules usually increase annually in April. The rates listed here are those that apply in 2025/26.

Adult disability payment

Adult disability payment is a benefit for adults who live in Scotland and have care needs and/or mobility problems because of a disability or long-term health condition. It is paid by Social Security Scotland. It is not affected by your income or capital and you do not have to have paid national insurance contributions.

Adult disability payment has replaced personal independence payment in Scotland. It is now available for all new claims. People who are still getting personal independence payment in Scotland will be transferred over to adult disability payment without having to make a new claim.

Who can claim?

You qualify for adult disability payment if all of the following apply.

- You are aged at least 16 and under pension age (although in limited circumstances you can claim after pension age).
- You are resident in Scotland and are not a person subject to immigration control.
- You meet the disability conditions for the daily living component and/or the mobility component.
- You are not entitled to child disability payment, disability living allowance, personal independence payment, attendance allowance or armed forces independence payment.

Adult disability payment has two components: one for daily living and the other for mobility. You can qualify for one or both. The daily living component is paid if you have problems with daily living activities, such as preparing food, washing and bathing, communicating and engaging with other people. The mobility component is paid if you have difficulty with your mobility, including planning and following journeys and moving around. You get points for how difficult you find each activity. The two components are paid at different rates, depending on how many points you score.

How much do you get?

Daily living component

Standard rate: £73.90 a week.

Enhanced rate: £110.40 a week.

Mobility component

Standard rate: £29.20 a week.

Enhanced rate: £77.05 a week.

How do you claim?

You can claim online at mygov.scot/adult-disability-payment/how-to-apply, by phoning Social Security Scotland on 0800 182 2222 to request a paper claim form or, if you use British Sign Language, via Contact Scotland BSL.

Special rules apply for people who are classed as terminally ill. See CPAG's *Welfare Benefits Handbook* for more information.

Attendance allowance

Attendance allowance is a benefit paid by the DWP to people who have care needs as a result of their disability and who are pension age or over when they claim. It is not affected by your income or capital, and you do not have to have paid national insurance contributions.

Note: in Scotland, attendance allowance is replaced by pension age disability payment.

Who can claim?

You qualify if all of the following apply.

- You have reached pension age.
- You live in England or Wales and satisfy conditions about residence and presence in the UK and you are not a person subject to immigration control.
- You satisfy a disability test. This tests whether you need help with your bodily functions or require supervision to avoid substantial danger to yourself or others. Depending on the amount of help you need, you may qualify for a lower or higher rate.

How much do you get?

Lower rate: £73.90 a week.

Higher rate: £110.40 a week.

How do you claim?

Claim on Form AA1, available from the DWP Attendance Allowance helpline on 0800 731 0122 (Relay UK dial 18001 first; textphone 0800 731 0317; British Sign Language services available). Requesting a form on the helpline is the best way to secure the earliest date for your claim, but you can also download a claim form at gov.uk/attendance-allowance/how-to-claim.

Special rules apply for people who are classed as terminally ill. See CPAG's *Welfare Benefits Handbook* for more information.

Bereavement benefits

Bereavement benefits are benefits paid by the DWP to widows, widowers, surviving civil partners and surviving cohabiting partners with children.

Bereavement benefits are not affected by your income or capital. Your late spouse or partner must have satisfied certain national insurance contribution conditions or died as the result of an industrial accident or disease.

If your spouse or partner died on or after 6 April 2017, you may be able to claim bereavement support payment. If your spouse or partner died before 6 April 2017 and you have been left to care for a child, you may still be able to get widowed parent's allowance instead.

Who can claim?

You qualify for **bereavement support payment** if all of the following apply.

- You are under pension age.
- Your spouse or partner died on or after 6 April 2017 (to be entitled for the maximum 18-month period, you must claim within three months of the death; to be entitled at all, you must claim within 21 months of the death).
- Your spouse or partner had either paid sufficient national insurance contributions or was employed and died as the result of an industrial injury or disease.
- You meet certain residence conditions.

It is paid for a maximum of 18 months.

You qualify for **widowed parent's allowance** if all of the following apply.

- You are under pension age. You have not remarried, entered into a civil partnership or started living with another person as if you were married or in a civil partnership.
- Your spouse or partner died before 6 April 2017.

- Your spouse or partner either had a sufficient national insurance record or was employed and died as the result of an industrial accident or disease.
- You are entitled to child benefit for a child and your late partner was their parent.

How much do you get?

Bereavement support payment

Initial lump sum: £2,500 standard rate; £3,500 higher rate.

Monthly amount: £100 standard rate; £350 higher rate.

You get the higher rate if you had children or were pregnant when your spouse or partner died.

Widowed parent's allowance

£150.90 a week. The rate is reduced if your late spouse or partner had an incomplete national insurance record.

How do you claim?

Claim by phoning the DWP's Bereavement Service on 0800 151 2012 (Relay UK dial 18001 first; Welsh language 0800 731 0453; textphone 0800 731 0464; British Sign Language services available).

Alternatively, you can use a claim form. For bereavement support payment, use Form BSP1, available from gov.uk/bereavement-support-payment/how-to-claim. There are two forms for widowed parent's allowance: use Form BB1 if you are a spouse or civil partner and use Form BB2 if you are a cohabiting partner. You can find both at gov.uk/widowed-parents-allowance/how-to-claim.

Best Start foods

Best Start foods (in Scotland) can help with your food costs if you are pregnant or have a child under age three. You get a payment card to spend on food including milk, plain fresh and frozen fruit and vegetables, pulses, eggs and infant formula milk. You can also get free vitamins. If you are in England or Wales, see the Healthy Start section.

Who can claim?

You qualify for Best Start foods if you or your partner are pregnant or responsible for a child under age three and you get universal credit (regardless of earnings), pension credit or housing benefit. If you are under 18, or aged 18 or 19 and a dependant (someone else is claiming chld benefit for you), you qualify even if you do not get any of these benefits.

You may also qualify if you have no recourse to public funds due to your immigration status and have a child under age three, depending on your income, regardless of the child's nationality.

How much do you get?

£5.40 a week during pregnancy, £10.80 a week for each child aged under one and £5.40 a week for each child aged one or two.

How do you claim?

Claim on the form (online or downloadable) at mygov.scot/best-start-grant-best-start-foods, by phoning Social Security Scotland on 0800 182 2222 or, if you use British Sign Language, via Contact Scotland BSL.

Best Start grant

Best Start grant is made up of three one-off payments to help with the costs of having a child. It is only available in Scotland and is paid by Social Security Scotland. If you are in England or Wales, see the information on Sure Start maternity grants.

To qualify for a Best Start grant, you must meet the following basic rules.

- You are ordinarily resident in Scotland.
- You are under 18, or age 18 or 19 and a dependant (someone else is still getting child benefit for you); or you or your partner are getting one or more of the following qualifying benefits:
  - universal credit (including if your award ended within the last month)
  - income-related employment and support allowance
  - pension credit
  - housing benefit
- You meet the conditions for the pregnancy and baby payment, the early learning payment or the school age payment.

Box A

Are you responsible for a child?

You are responsible for a child for the Best Start grant and Best Start foods if any of the following applies on the day you claim.

- The child is your dependant. They count as your dependant if you get child benefit for them or they are included in your universal credit or pension credit award.
- You are under 20, the parent of the child, you normally live with them and you are a dependant in someone else's child benefit, universal credit or pension credit.
- You have adopted the child under Scottish law, or under the law of another jurisdiction recognised under Scottish law.
- The child has been placed with you for adoption and you are then appointed as their guardian.
- You are a kinship carer and the child lives with you under a kinship care order or an agreement with a local authority.
- You have a parental order following a surrogate pregnancy.

Who can claim a pregnancy and baby payment?

This is a grant to help with the costs of having a new baby.

You must meet the basic rules for a Best Start grant. You can qualify from the 24th week of pregnancy up to six months after the baby is born (including if the baby is stillborn or dies within this period).

You may also qualify if you become responsible for a baby who is under the age of one – eg, as a kinship carer or where a child is placed with you for adoption. You have to claim before the child's first birthday.

Who can claim an early learning payment?

This is a grant to help with the costs of having a young child aged between two and three and a half.

You must meet the basic rules for a Best Start grant and you must be responsible for the child (see Box A). You must claim between the child's second birthday and the date six months after their third birthday.

Who can claim a school age payment?

This is a grant to help with the costs of a child reaching school age.

You must meet the basic rules for a Best Start grant and be responsible for the child (see Box A).

You are eligible from the start of June in the year your child is able to start school, to the end of the following February, but they need not have actually started school. If your child's date of birth falls between 1 March 2020 and 28 February 2021 (inclusive), you have to claim between 1 June 2025 and 28 February 2026. If your child's date of birth falls between 1 March 2021 and 29 February 2022 (inclusive), you have to claim between 1 June 2026 and 28 February 2027.

How much do you get?

Pregnancy and baby payment: £767.50 (or £383.75 if you have another child under 16). You can still get the higher rate if you have another child in some situations, such as if you have left domestic abuse or you are a refugee and already had an older child when you came to the UK.

Early learning payment: £319.80.

School age payment: £319.80.

How do you claim?

Use the form (online or downloadable) at mygov.scot/best-start-grant, or claim by phoning Social Security Scotland on 0800 182 2222 or, if you use British Sign Language, via Contact Scotland BSL. If you get Scottish child payment for the child, the early learning payment and school age payment may be made automatically.

Carer's allowance

Carer's allowance is a benefit paid by the DWP to people who spend at least 35 hours a week looking after a disabled adult or disabled child. Temporary breaks in caring are allowed in certain circumstances. If you are working, you must not be earning more than £196 a week. Otherwise, it is not affected by your income or capital, and you do not have to have paid national insurance contributions. **Note:** in Scotland, carer's allowance is being replaced by carer support payment. People still getting carer's allowance in Scotland are being transferred to carer support payment without having to make a new claim.

Who can claim?

You qualify if all of the following apply.

- You are aged at least 16.
- You are caring for a person who is receiving:

  - attendance allowance
  - either the highest or the middle care component rate of disability living allowance or child disability payment
  - either rate of the daily living component of personal independence payment or adult disability payment
  - armed forces independence payment
  - constant attendance allowance with an industrial injury benefit or war pension
- You are providing care for at least 35 hours a week.
- You are not earning more than £196 a week.
- You are not a full-time student.
- You live in England or Wales, satisfy certain residence conditions and are not a person subject to immigration control.

How much do you get?

£83.30 a week.

How do you claim?

Claim online at gov.uk/carers-allowance/how-to-claim or download Form DS700 (Form DS700(SP) if you get a state pension). You can also claim by phoning the Carer's Allowance Unit on 0800 731 0297 (Relay UK dial 18001 first; textphone 0800 731 0317; British Sign Language services available).

Carer support payment

Carer support payment is a benefit paid by Social Security Scotland to people who spend at least 35 hours a week looking after a disabled adult or disabled child. Temporary breaks in caring are allowed in certain circumstances. If you are working, you must not be earning more than £196 a week. Otherwise, it is not affected by your income or capital, and you do not have to have paid national insurance contributions.

Carer support payment replaces carer's allowance in Scotland. You can no longer make a new claim for carer's allowance in Scotland.

Who can claim?

You qualify if all of the following apply.

- You are aged at least 16.
- You are caring for a person who is receiving:
  - attendance allowance or pension age disability payment
  - either the highest or the middle care component rate of child disability payment, disability living allowance or Scottish adult disability living allowance
  - either rate of the daily living component of personal independence payment or adult disability payment
  - armed forces independence payment
  - constant attendance allowance with an industrial injury benefit or war pension
- You are providing care for at least 35 hours a week.
- You are not earning more than £196 a week.
- You live in Scotland, satisfy certain residence conditions and are not a person subject to immigration control.

How much do you get?

£83.30 a week.

If you get carer support payment, you are also entitled to a carer's allowance supplement. This is usually paid twice a year as a lump-sum payment. In 2025, the payments are £293.50 each. You must be getting carer support payment or carer's allowance on a qualifying date. The supplement does not affect your other benefits. At the time of writing, carer's allowance supplement was due be replaced by Scottish carer supplement in 2026.

How do you claim?

Claim online at mygov.scot/carer-support-payment/how-to-apply, by phoning Social Security Scotland on 0800 182 2222 to request a paper claim form or, if you use British Sign Language, via Contact Scotland BSL.

Child benefit

Child benefit is a benefit paid by HM Revenue and Customs to people who are responsible for a child. It is paid for each child for whom you are responsible, with a higher amount paid for the eldest child. You do not have to be the child's parent. Child benefit is not affected by your income or capital, and you do not have to have paid national insurance contributions. If you or your partner have an individual annual income of over £60,000, you may pay additional income tax to recover the child benefit.

Who can claim?

You qualify if all of the following apply.

- The child counts as either a child or a qualifying young person for the purposes of child benefit. This includes all children under 16, and those aged between 16 and 19 in non-advanced education at school or college (eg, studying GCSEs, AS and A levels, NVQ level 3 or below, Scottish National Qualifications up to Higher or Advanced Higher level or for a BTEC) for more than 12 hours a week, or those aged between 16 and 19 in approved training.
- You are responsible for the child. The child must live with you, or you must contribute at least the rate of child benefit to the cost of supporting them.
- You have priority over anyone else. If someone else tries to claim child benefit, you have priority if the child lives with you, if you are the wife and you are living with your husband, or you are the child's mother and you are not married to your partner.
- You and the child satisfy certain presence and residence conditions, and you are not a person subject to immigration control.
- The child is not getting universal credit in their own right.

In certain circumstances, you cannot get child benefit, including if the child is being looked after by a local authority, is living as part of a couple, or is in prison or other custody.

How much do you get?

Only or eldest child: £26.05 a week.

Other child(ren): £17.25 a week.

There is no limit to the number of children you can get child benefit for.

How do you claim?

Claim online or on Form CH2 (and CH2 (CS) for additional children), downloadable from gov.uk/child-benefit/how-to-claim or from the HM Revenue and Customs Child Benefit Office on 0300 200 3100 (Relay UK dial 18001 first; Welsh language 0300 200 1900).

Child disability payment

Child disability payment is a benefit for children in Scotland who have care needs and/or mobility problems because of a disability. It is only available in Scotland and is paid by Social Security Scotland. It is not affected by your income or capital, and you do not have to have paid national insurance contributions.

Child disability payment has replaced disability living allowance for children and young people in Scotland. You can no longer make a new claim for disability living allowance in Scotland.

Who can claim?

In most cases, claims are made for the child by their parent or someone with authority to act on their behalf. The child will qualify if all of the following apply.

- The child is younger than 16 when you first claim (when the child turns 16, they will normally be expected to manage the claim from then on; entitlement can continue until 18).
- The child meets the conditions about residence in Scotland and presence in Great Britain, and is not a person subject to immigration control.
- The child satisfies a disability test.
  - If the child needs help with care needs, the disability test looks at whether the child needs help with their bodily functions, or whether they require supervision to avoid substantial danger to themself or others. Depending on the amount of help the child needs, they may qualify for one of three rates.
  - If the child needs help with mobility problems, the test looks at whether they are virtually unable to walk or have certain severe disabilities (for the higher rate), or whether they need guidance or supervision to walk (for the lower rate). A child must be at least three years old to get the higher rate of the mobility component and at least five to get the lower rate.

A child must need substantially more help than a child of the same age without a disability would need.

How much do you get?

Care component

Lowest rate: £29.20 a week.

Middle rate: £73.90 a week.

Highest rate: £110.40 a week.

Mobility component

Lower rate: £29.20 a week.

Higher rate: £77.05 a week.

How do you claim?

You can claim on the form (online or downloadable) at mygov.scot/child-disability-payment/how-to-apply, by phoning Social Security Scotland on 0800 182 2222 or, if you use British Sign Language, via Contact Scotland BSL, or by post using the downloaded form (which Social Security Scotland can also send to you on request).

Special rules apply for people who are classed as terminally ill. See CPAG's *Welfare Benefits Handbook* for more information.

Cold weather payments

Cold weather payments are paid to people in England and Wales when freezing temperature is forecast or recorded in their area for seven days in a row. If you are in Scotland, see the section on winter heating payments.

You must be getting one of the following benefits:

- universal credit
- income-related employment and support allowance
- pension credit

If you get universal credit, you must have a child under age five or a child getting a disability benefit, or you have limited capability for work, and you must not be in employment or gainful self-employment during the period of cold weather.

You do not need to make a claim for cold weather payments. The DWP pays you automatically if you qualify.

Council tax reduction

Council tax reduction is help with council tax for people on a low income. It reduces the amount of council tax you have to pay – it is not a payment of money. The reduction in your council tax is made by your local authority.

It is separate from council tax discounts and exemptions, which you may qualify for due to your circumstances.

Who can claim?

You qualify if all of the following apply.

- You or your partner are liable for council tax for the home in which you live.
- You satisfy the habitual residence test and the right to reside test and you are not a person subject to immigration control.
- Your savings are sufficiently low.
- Your income is sufficiently low.

How much is the reduction?

The amount of council tax reduction you get depends on your circumstances. In England and Wales, local authorities may have their own way of calculating what help you can get. In Scotland, there is a national scheme applied by all local authorities. In all the schemes, the local authority takes into account things like your household income and how many other adults and children live with you.

How do you claim?

Claim from your local authority. You can use the postcode finder at gov.uk/apply-council-tax-reduction to find your local authority's website and information about council tax reduction.

Disability living allowance

Disability living allowance is a benefit paid by the DWP to people who have care needs and/or mobility problems because of a disability. It is not affected by income or capital, and you do not have to have paid national insurance contributions.

New claims can now only be made for children under 16. Disability living allowance for adults is replaced by personal independence payment. If you still get disability living allowance, at some point you will have your award reassessed to see whether you qualify for personal independence payment.

Note: in Scotland, disability living allowance for children aged under 16 is replaced by child disability payment and disability living allowance for adults is replaced by adult disability payment (or in some cases, Scottish adult disability living allowance).

Who can claim?

You qualify if all of the following apply.

- You are aged under 16 when you (or someone claiming for you, usually your parent) first claim.
- You live in England or Wales and meet certain conditions about residence and presence in the UK and you are not a person subject to immigration control.
- You satisfy a disability test.
  - If you need help with your care needs, the disability test looks at whether you need help with your bodily functions or whether you require supervision to avoid substantial danger to yourself or others. Depending on the amount of help you need, you may qualify for one of three rates.
  - If you need help with mobility problems, the test looks at whether you are virtually unable to walk or have certain severe disabilities (for the higher rate), or whether you need guidance or supervision to walk (for the lower rate). A child must be at least three years old to get the higher rate of the mobility component and at least five to get the lower rate.

A child must need substantially more help than a child of the same age without a disability would need.

How much do you get?

Care component

Lowest rate: £29.20 a week.

Middle rate: £73.90 a week.

Highest rate: £110.40 a week.

Mobility component

Lower rate: £29.20 a week.

Higher rate: £77.05 a week.

How do you claim?

Claim on Form DLA1A Child, available from the DWP Disability Living Allowance helpline on 0800 121 4600 (Relay UK dial 18001 first; textphone 0800 121 4523) or from gov.uk/disability-living-allowance-children/how-to-claim. It is best to request the form from the helpline as the claim is dated from the date of your call if you complete and return it within six weeks.

Special rules apply for people who are classed as terminally ill. See CPAG's *Welfare Benefits Handbook* for more information.

Discretionary housing payments

Discretionary housing payments are extra payments that your local authority can make if you need help with your housing costs. You must be entitled to housing benefit or help with your rent in your universal credit to get discretionary housing payments.

The local authority has discretion whether or not to pay you, how much to pay you and over what period.

In Scotland, you should always be able to get a discretionary housing payment if you are affected by the bedroom tax or benefit cap.

Employment and support allowance

Employment and support allowance (also called new-style employment and support allowance) is a benefit paid by the DWP to people who cannot work because of illness or disability. This is known as having limited capability for work and the DWP assesses it using a test called the work capability assessment.

This benefit is for people unable to work who have paid sufficient national insurance contributions to qualify. It is not affected by most types of income and capital. New-style employment and support allowance is not being replaced by universal credit; you can get it at the same time but it counts as income in full for universal credit.

Box B

Income-related (old-style) employment and support allowance

Income-related (also called old-style) employment and support allowance is for people unable to work and who are on a low income. Your entitlement is affected by your income and capital, but you do not need to have paid national insurance contributions.

This benefit is being abolished and replaced by universal credit. You cannot make a new claim for income-related employment and support allowance. The government is notifying everyone getting income-related employment and support allowance that they need to claim universal credit instead. The government intends to have notified everyone by September 2025 and stopped all income-related employment and support allowance awards by the end of March 2026.

Who can claim?

You qualify for employment and support allowance if all of the following apply.

- You have limited capability for work.
- You are aged at least 16 and under pension age
- You are in Great Britain.
- You are not getting jobseeker's allowance or statutory sick pay.
- You satisfy certain national insurance contribution conditions, including having paid sufficient class 1 or class 2 contributions in one of the last two recent tax years before the year of your claim

– so you must have been working at least at some point in those years.
- You are not working (although work is permitted if it is less than 16 hours a week and you earn no more than £195.50 a week).

How much do you get?

You get an amount for yourself. Amounts for your partner and children are not included. There is a basic amount during an initial assessment phase (usually 13 weeks) of £72.90 a week if you are aged under 25, or £92.05 if you are aged 25 or over. After the assessment phase, the basic amount is £92.05 in all cases. An additional support component of £48.50 is then included if you are assessed as being so ill or disabled that you are not required to undertake any work-related activity. The DWP calls this the support group. Before 3 April 2017, claimants who were assessed as not being in the support group got an additional amount (a work-related activity component), now worth £36.55, included. If you were entitled to this component, you continue to get it.

How do you claim?

Claim at gov.uk/how-to-claim-new-style-esa. If you cannot claim online, phone the Jobcentre Plus new claims helpline on 0800 055 6688 (Relay UK dial 18001 first; Welsh language 0800 328 1744; textphone 0800 328 1344; British Sign Language services available).

Funeral expenses payment

A funeral expenses payment is a lump sum to cover the basic costs of a funeral plus some other related expenses in England and Wales. If you are in Scotland, see the information about funeral support payment. In addition, in England there is a children's funeral payment to cover the reasonable costs of a funeral of a child aged under 18 or a stillborn child born after the 24th week of pregnancy. The person providing the funeral applies for a children's funeral payment – ie, the funeral director in most cases.

Who can claim?

You qualify for a funeral expenses payment if all of the following apply:

- You live in England or Wales.
- You or your partner are responsible for the funeral costs. If your child or partner has died, you are responsible for the funeral costs. If you are a close relative or friend of the deceased, it must be reasonable for you to have accepted responsibility for the funeral costs. There are also rules that exclude some people from claiming if someone else, not on benefit, could have paid for the funeral.
- You or your partner are getting one of the following qualifying benefits:
  - universal credit
  - income-related employment and support allowance
  - housing benefit
  - pension credit
- The person who has died was ordinarily resident in the UK.
- The funeral takes place in the UK, but in limited circumstances a funeral in a European Economic Area state or Switzerland may be accepted.
- You claim within six months of the funeral.

How much do you get?

The funeral expenses payment does not usually cover the full costs of a funeral. It covers the cost of a burial plot, necessary burial fees and cremation fees. It also covers the costs of any medical certificates required and any documentation required for the release of the assets of the person who has died. You can get certain transport costs and up to £1,000 for other funeral expenses. The payment may be reduced by the amount of assets of the person who has died, or an amount under a funeral plan, insurance policy, occupational pension scheme or equivalent paid on the person's death, or may be recovered from the estate of the person who has died.

How do you claim?

Start your claim for a funeral expenses payment by phoning the Bereavement Service on 0800 151 2012 (Relay UK dial 18001 first; Welsh language 0800 731 0453; textphone 0800 731 0464; British Sign Language services available). If you want to use a claim form (Form SF200), you can download this from gov.uk/funeral-payments/how-to-claim or ask for it to be sent to you.

Funeral support payment

A funeral support payment is a one-off payment to help with the costs of a funeral. It is only available in Scotland and is paid by Social Security Scotland. If you are in England or Wales, see the information about funeral expenses payment.

Who can claim?

You qualify if all of the following apply.

- You normally live in Scotland.
- You or your partner get one of the following qualifying benefits:
  - universal credit (including if your award ended in the last month)
  - income-related employment and support allowance
  - pension credit
  - housing benefit
- You or your partner have accepted responsibility for the funeral costs and it is reasonable for you to do so. Usually, it will be reasonable for the person with the closest family relationship to the person who has died to accept responsibility, but other factors, such as estrangement, may also be relevant.
- The person who has died was ordinarily resident in the UK.
- The funeral takes place in the UK (but in limited circumstances a funeral outside the UK may qualify).
- You claim within six months of the funeral.

How much do you get?

The funeral support payment does not usually cover the full costs of a funeral. It covers the cost of a burial plot, necessary burial fees and cremation fees. It also covers the costs of any medical certificates required and any documentation required for the release of the assets of the person who has died. You can get £1,279.15 towards other funeral expenses. The funeral support payment may be reduced by the amount of assets of the person who has died, or an amount under a funeral plan, insurance policy, occupational pension scheme or equivalent paid on the person's death, or may be recovered from the estate of the person who has died.

How do you claim?

Claim at mygov.scot/funeral-support-payment, by phoning Social Security Scotland on 0800 182 2222 or on a claim form which you can download or request by phone.

Guardian's allowance

Guardian's allowance is a benefit paid by HM Revenue and Customs to people looking after a child who is, in effect, an orphan. Your entitlement is not affected by your income or capital, and you do not have to have paid national insurance contributions.

Who can claim?

You qualify if the following apply.

- You are entitled to child benefit for the child.
- The child is an orphan, or one of their parents has died and all reasonable efforts to trace the other parent have been unsuccessful or they are in prison or detained in hospital.

How much do you get?

£22.10 a week (this is the amount per child, if more than one).

How do you claim?

Claim on Form BG1, available from the Guardian's Allowance Unit on 0300 322 9080 or downloadable from gov.uk/guardians-allowance/how-to-claim.

Health benefits

Health benefits can provide help with the costs of NHS prescriptions, dental treatment, sight tests and glasses, wigs and fabric supports, as well as fares to receive NHS treatment. The help available is providing such items free or at a reduced cost – health benefits are not payments of money. They are awarded by the NHS Business Services Authority.

In Wales and Scotland, prescriptions, wigs and fabric supports are provided free of charge. Sight tests and NHS dental check-ups are also free in Scotland.

Who can claim?

You qualify if you are in an exempt group, so you get the item free of charge. You are in an exempt group if you get universal credit (with monthly earnings under £435, or £935 if you have children or a health condition), income-related employment and support allowance or the guarantee credit of pension credit. Other people in exempt groups include young people in education, care leavers, pregnant women and asylum seekers.

Alternatively, you qualify if you are on a low income, so that you get the item at reduced cost. Whether or not you qualify depends on your circumstances, including how much income you have.

How do you claim?

Ask at your dentist, optician or hospital about exemption. If you are in an exempt group, you are usually asked to complete the back of the prescription form or another appropriate form. If you are not exempt, claim help under the low income scheme on Form HC1, available from GP practices, dentists, opticians, some chemists and advice centres, or apply online at services.nhsbsa.nhs.uk/apply-for-help-with-nhs-costs/apply-online.

Healthy Start

Healthy Start (in England and Wales) can help with your food costs if you are pregnant or have a child under four.

Healthy Start provides a payment card to spend on food including milk, plain fresh and frozen fruit and vegetables, pulses and infant formula milk. You can also get free vitamins.

Note: In Scotland, Healthy Start has been replaced by Best Start foods.

Who can claim?

You qualify for Healthy Start if the following apply.

- You are at least 10 weeks pregnant or you have a child aged under four; **and if you are aged 18 or over**, you or a member of your family get universal credit with earnings of no more than £408 a month, or income-related employment and support allowance or pension credit.
- **If you are under 18 and pregnant**, you qualify even if you do not get any of the benefits mentioned above.
- If you have no recourse to public funds due to your immigration status, you may also qualify, depending on your income, if the child is a British citizen.

How much do you get?

£4.25 a week during pregnancy, £8.50 a week for each child aged under one and £4.25 for each child from age one until their fourth birthday.

How do you claim?

Claim on the form in the Healthy Start leaflet (HS01) available from midwives, health visitors, maternity clinics and doctors' surgeries, or by phoning 0300 330 7010 or emailing healthy.start@nhsbsa.nhs.uk. Alternatively, claim online at healthystart.nhs.uk/how-to-apply.

Housing benefit

Housing benefit is for people in temporary or supported accommodation, or over pension age, on a low income who need help paying their rent. It is paid by your local authority. You can find your local authority at gov.uk/find-local-council. Your entitlement is affected by your income and capital, but you do not need to have paid national insurance contributions.

Who can claim?

You can only get housing benefit in limited circumstances.

You can get it **if you are at least pension age**. If you are in a couple, usually both you and your partner must be of pension age. If one of you is below pension age, usually you cannot make a new claim for housing benefit, unless you were at least pension age on 14 May 2019 and were entitled as a couple to pension credit or housing benefit (or both) and are still entitled to one or both of those benefits as part of the same couple.

You can also get housing benefit **if you are in specified supported accommodation** where you get care, support or supervision, or a refuge, or you are in temporary homeless accommodation.

You qualify if all of the following apply.

- You or your partner are liable to pay rent for your home.
- You are not excluded from entitlement. Most full-time students cannot get housing benefit, although lone parents, some couples with children and some students with disabilities can. People living in care homes and those considered not to be renting on a commercial basis are also excluded.

- You satisfy the habitual residence test and the right to reside test, and are not a person subject to immigration control.
- You do not have more than £16,000 capital (unless you also get the guarantee credit of pension credit) and your income is sufficiently low.

How much do you get?

Housing benefit might not cover your rent in full. The actual amount you get depends on your circumstances, including the amount of your rent, your income and capital (including your partner's income and capital), and whether anyone else is living in your home. Some service charges you pay to your landlord on top of your rent may also be included.

The local authority also takes into account how many bedrooms you need and the local housing allowance for your area – see lha-direct.voa.gov.uk/bedroomcalculator.aspx. The DWP provides links to independent benefit calculators at gov.uk/benefits-calculators.

If you are working age, you can only get housing benefit in temporary or specified supported accommodation, and this is not affected by the local housing allowance, bedroom tax or benefit cap.

If you are pension age, you are not affected by the bedroom tax or benefit cap, but may be affected by the local housing allowance in private rented accommodation.

Industrial injuries benefits

Industrial injuries benefits are paid by the DWP to people who are disabled as a result of an accident at work or an industrial disease. The main benefit is **industrial injuries disablement benefit**.

Industrial injuries benefits are not affected by your income or capital, and you do not have to have paid national insurance contributions.

Who can claim?

You qualify if all of the following apply.

- You have had a personal injury in an accident at work, or you have a prescribed industrial disease.
- At the time of the injury you were an employee, or your disease was caused by your work as an employee.
- As a result of that injury or disease, you are assessed as having a sufficient level of disablement.

See gov.uk/industrial-injuries-disablement-benefit for more information.

How much do you get?

You get industrial injuries benefit for yourself. Amounts for your partner and children are not included. The amount you get depends on the extent of your disablement.

How do you claim?

Request a claim form by phoning Barnsley Industrial Injuries Disablement Benefit Centre on 0800 121 8379 (Relay UK dial 18001 first; textphone 0800 169 0314) or download a form from gov.uk/industrial-injuries-disablement-benefit/how-to-claim.

Job Start Payment

Job Start Payment is paid by Social Security Scotland to young people who are starting work. You need to have been out of work and getting universal credit.

Who can claim?

You qualify for Job Start Payment if all the following apply.

- You live in Scotland.

- You are aged at least 16 and under 25 on the date you get the job offer.
- You are starting work averaging at least 12 hours a week over a four-week period.
- You have been out of work and getting universal credit for six months.

If you are a care leaver aged at least 16 and under 26, you can get Job Start Payment if you are getting universal credit when you are offered the job; you do not need to have been getting it for six months.

How much do you get?

Job Start Payment is a one-off payment of £319.80. If you are responsible for a child, you will get a higher payment of £511.65.

How do you claim?

Claim online at mygov.scot/job-start-payment, by phoning Social Security Scotland on 0800 182 2222 or on a claim form which you can download or request by phone.

Jobseeker's allowance

Jobseeker's allowance (also known as new-style jobseeker's allowance) is for people looking for work who have paid sufficient national insurance contributions to qualify. It is not affected by your capital or income, other than your earnings or any occupational or personal pension you have. Your earnings are taken into account in full, except for a disregard of, usually, £5 a week. The first £50 a week of your occupational or personal pension is ignored, but amounts above that are taken into account.

You can get jobseeker's allowance while getting universal credit, although it counts as income in full for universal credit.

Who can claim?

You qualify if all of the following apply.

- You are unemployed or are working less than 16 hours a week.
- You do not have limited capability for work – ie, you are not considered too ill to work.
- You satisfy the jobseeking conditions – ie, you must be available for and actively seeking work. If you come under the universal credit system, you must satisfy the work-related requirements.
- You satisfy the national insurance contribution conditions. These include having paid sufficient class 1 or class 2 contributions in one of the last two recent tax years before the year of your claim, so you need to have been working at least at some point in those years.
- You are under pension age.
- You are in Great Britain.

How much do you get?

You get an amount for yourself. Amounts for your partner and children are not included. The amount depends on your age.

Under 25: £72.90 a week.

25 or over: £92.05 a week.

How do you claim?

Claim online at gov.uk/jobseekers-allowance/apply-new-style-jsa. If you need help or cannot claim online, claim by phoning Jobcentre Plus on 0800 055 6688 (Relay UK dial 18001 first; Welsh language 0800 012 1888; textphone 0800 023 4888; British Sign Language services available).

Local welfare assistance

Local authorities can pay local welfare assistance to people in need – eg, to ease exceptional pressure on a family or following a crisis. This may be in the form of a grant or a loan. In England, local authorities have the discretion to make their own rules. In Scotland, the Scottish Welfare Fund, paid through your local authority, provides grants, vouchers or goods. In Wales, the Discretionary Assistance Fund for Wales, paid through your local authority, also offers non-repayable payments.

How do you claim?

Contact your local authority. It will tell you claim procedures. You can find your local authority at gov.uk/find-local-council.

Maternity allowance

Maternity allowance is a benefit paid by the DWP to women who are pregnant or who have recently given birth and who have worked during pregnancy but are not entitled to statutory maternity pay. It is not affected by your income or capital, and you do not need to have paid national insurance contributions.

Who can claim?

You qualify if all of the following apply.

- You are pregnant or have recently given birth and are within your maternity allowance period. This is a period of 39 weeks (in some cases, 14 weeks) starting, at the earliest, 11 weeks before the week in which your baby is due.
- You were working for at least 26 weeks in the 66 weeks immediately before the week in which your baby is due, or you assisted your spouse or civil partner with their self-employment in at least 26 weeks of those 66 weeks (in this case, your maternity allowance period is 14 weeks rather than 39).
- Your average gross earnings in the 66 weeks immediately before the week in which your baby is due were at least £30 a week (if you were working).
- You are not entitled to statutory maternity pay.

There is an official calculator for working out your eligibility at gov.uk/maternity-paternity-pay-leave.

How much do you get?

£187.18 a week (or 90 per cent of your average weekly earnings, if less).

If you qualify because you help with your spouse's or civil partner's self-employment: £27 a week.

How do you claim?

Claim on Form MA1, available online at gov.uk/maternity-allowance/how-to-claim. If you cannot print a copy of the form, follow the online prompts to order a form or phone the Jobcentre Plus national contact centre on 0800 055 6688 (Relay UK dial 18001 first; Welsh language 0800 012 1888; textphone 0800 023 4888; British Sign Language services available) to ask for a copy to be sent to you.

Pension age disability payment

Pension age disability payment is a benefit paid by Social Security Scotland to people in Scotland who have care needs as a result of their disability and who are pension age or over when they claim. It is not affected by your income or capital, and you do not have to have paid national insurance contributions.

Who can claim?

You qualify if all of the following apply.

- You have reached pension age.
- You satisfy conditions about residence and presence in Scotland and you are not a person subject to immigration control.
- You satisfy a disability test. This tests whether you need help with your bodily functions or require supervision to avoid substantial

danger to yourself or others. Depending on the amount of help you need, you may qualify for a lower or higher rate.

How much do you get?

Lower rate: £73.90 a week.

Higher rate: £110.40 a week.

How do you claim?

You can claim online at mygov.scot/pension-age-disability-payment/how-to-apply, by phoning Social Security Scotland on 0800 182 2222 to request a paper claim form or, if you use British Sign Language, via Contact Scotland BSL.

Special rules apply for people who are classed as terminally ill. See CPAG's *Welfare Benefits Handbook* for more information.

Pension credit

Pension credit is a benefit paid by the DWP to people who have reached pension age and who are on a low income. Your entitlement is affected by your income, but you do not need to have paid national insurance contributions.

Pension credit has two elements: a guarantee credit, which brings your income up to a minimum level, and a savings credit, which is for people who reached pension age before 6 April 2016 and whose income is at least a certain level. Savings credit is being phased out and you cannot now qualify for it if you reach pension age after that date.

Who can claim?

You qualify for the guarantee credit of pension credit if all of the following apply.

- You have reached pension age.
- Your income is low enough.

- Your partner is not already entitled to pension credit. If your partner has not reached pension age, see below.
- You are in Great Britain, you satisfy the habitual residence test and the right to reside test, and you are not a person subject to immigration control.

You can check your pension age at gov.uk/state-pension-age. It is 66 at the time of writing, but is gradually rising if you were born after 6 April 1960.

If your partner has not reached pension age, usually you cannot make a new claim for pension credit, unless on 14 May 2019 you were, as part of the same couple, entitled to pension credit or housing benefit for people of pension age (or both), and are still entitled to one or both of those benefits as part of the same couple.

How much do you get?

Pension credit ensures your income is at least £227.10 a week as a single person or £346.60 a week for a couple.

The actual amount you get depends on your circumstances, including whether you have children, a severe disability or you are a carer, your income and (if you have capital of over £10,000) your capital. The circumstances (including the income and capital) of your partner are also taken into account. See an official calculator for working out how much you might get at gov.uk/pension-credit/what-youll-get.

How do you claim?

The DWP encourages you to start your claim by phoning the Pension Service on 0800 991 234 (Relay UK dial 18001 first; textphone 0800 169 0133; British Sign Language services available). Alternatively, you can use the claim form, Form PC1, which you can get from the Pension Service. If you have already claimed your state retirement pension and have no children, you can also claim online at gov.uk/pension-credit/how-to-claim.

Personal independence payment

Personal independence payment is a benefit paid by the DWP to people aged between 16 and pension age who have care needs and/or have mobility problems because of a disability. Your entitlement is not affected by your income or capital, and you do not have to have paid national insurance contributions.

Personal independence payment has replaced disability living allowance. Those already getting disability living allowance are having their awards transferred to personal independence payment. People over pension age who are claiming for the first time must claim attendance allowance instead.

Note: in Scotland, personal independence payment is being replaced by adult disability payment.

Who can claim?

You qualify if all of the following apply.

- You are aged between 16 and pension age.
- You satisfy certain conditions about residence in England or Wales and presence in the UK and are not a person subject to immigration control.
- You satisfy a disability test.

Personal independence payment has two components: one for problems with daily living activities, such as preparing food, washing and bathing, communicating and engaging with other people; and one for mobility activities, including planning and following journeys and moving around. You can receive one or both. You are given a certain number of points for the severity of your problems in each activity. You can get different rates of each component, depending on how many points you score.

How much do you get?

Daily living component

Standard rate: £73.90 a week.

Enhanced rate: £110.40 a week.

Mobility component

Standard rate: £29.20 a week.

Enhanced rate: £77.05 a week.

How do you claim?

Start your claim by phoning the claim line on 0800 917 2222 (Relay UK dial 18001 first; textphone 0800 917 7777; British Sign Language services available). A 'How your disability affects you' form is then sent to you. Different arrangements apply if you are unable to claim by phone or are terminally ill: see gov.uk/pip/how-to-claim.

Special rules apply for people who are classed as terminally ill. See CPAG's *Welfare Benefits Handbook* for more information.

Scottish child payment

Scottish child payment is a top-up to means-tested benefits for low-income families in Scotland with a child aged under 16. It is paid by Social Security Scotland.

Who can claim?

You qualify if all the following apply.

- You live in Scotland.
- You are responsible for a child aged under 16.
- You or your partner are entitled to one or more of the following qualifying benefits:
  - universal credit
  - income-related employment and support allowance
  - pension credit

You count as responsible for a child if you or your partner get child benefit for them, or an amount for them is included in your universal credit or pension credit, or you are their kinship carer.

How much do you get?

£27.15 a week for each child who qualifies.

How do you claim?

Claim on the form (online or downloadable) at mygov.scot/scottish-child-payment/how-to-apply, by phoning Social Security Scotland on 0800 182 2222 or, if you use British Sign Language, via Contact Scotland BSL.

Statutory adoption pay

Statutory adoption pay is paid by employers to their employees who are stopping work to adopt a child and who satisfy certain conditions about employment and earnings. Your entitlement is not affected by your income and capital.

Who can claim?

You qualify if all of the following apply.

- You are adopting a child.
- You have worked for your employer continuously for at least 26 weeks by the time you were matched with the child for adoption.
- Your average gross earnings are at least a certain level – £125 a week at the time of writing.
- You give the correct notice and proof of the adoption to your employer.
- You are in the adoption pay period – this is 39 weeks, usually beginning, at the earliest, 14 days before the day you expect the child to be placed with you and, at the latest, on the date of placement.

You can find information about the notice and proof at gov.uk/adoption-pay-leave/eligibility.

How much do you get?

First six weeks: 90 per cent of your average weekly earnings a week.

Remaining 33 weeks: £187.18 a week (or 90 per cent of your average weekly earnings, if less).

How do you claim?

Contact your employer. There is no claim form, but you must give your employer the correct notice and information.

Statutory maternity pay

Statutory maternity pay is paid by employers to their employees who are stopping work to have a baby, and who satisfy certain conditions about employment and earnings. Your entitlement is not affected by your income and capital.

Who can claim?

You qualify if all of the following apply.

- You are pregnant or have recently given birth.
- You have worked for your employer continuously for at least 26 weeks by the 15th week before the week in which your baby is due.
- Your average gross earnings are at least a certain level – £125 a week at the time of writing.
- You give the correct notice and proof of the pregnancy to your employer.
- You are in the maternity pay period – this is 39 weeks beginning, at the earliest, 11 weeks before the week in which your baby is due and, at the latest, the day after your baby is born.

You can find information about the notice and proof at gov.uk/maternity-pay-leave/how-to-claim.

How much do you get?

First six weeks: 90 per cent of your average weekly earnings a week.

Remaining 33 weeks: £187.18 a week (or 90 per cent of your average weekly earnings, if less).

How do you claim?

Contact your employer. There is no claim form, but you must give your employer the correct notice and information.

Statutory neonatal care pay

Statutory neonatal care pay is paid by employers to their employees who have a newborn baby undergoing hospital treatment, and who satisfy certain conditions about employment and earnings. Your entitlement is not affected by your income and capital. It is paid for up to 12 weeks.

Who can claim?

You qualify if all of the following apply.

- Your baby is undergoing hospital treatment for at least seven days starting within 28 days of the day after the birth. This can be in hospital or at home under the direction and monitoring of the hospital, or palliative end of life care.
- You have worked for your employer continuously for at least 26 weeks by the 15th week before the expected week of childbirth, or the week in which the neonatal care starts.
- Your average gross earnings are at least a certain level – £125 a week at the time of writing.

You are entitled to statutory neonatal care leave even if you do not meet the continuous employment and earnings conditions. If you are already on maternity, paternity or shared parental leave when your baby is in neonatal care, your statutory neonatal leave and pay can be taken after that period, within 68 weeks of the birth. If you have a partner, you can both qualify for statutory neonatal care pay of up to 12 weeks.

You can find information about the notice and proof at gov.uk/neonatal-care-pay-leave/how-to-claim.

How much do you get?

£187.18 a week (or 90 per cent of your average weekly earnings, if less).

How do you claim?

Contact your employer. There is no claim form, but you must give your employer the correct notice and information.

Statutory parental bereavement pay

Statutory parental bereavement pay is paid by employers to employees who meet certain conditions after the death of a child or a stillbirth. It is paid for up to two weeks.

Who can claim?

You qualify if all of the following apply.

- You are a bereaved parent following the death of a child aged under 18 or following a stillbirth after 24 weeks of pregnancy.
- You have been continuously employed by the same employer for at least 26 weeks up to the week in which the child died or was stillborn.
- Your average gross earnings are at least a certain level – £125 a week at the time of writing.
- You give your employer correct notice of the week or weeks in which you want the payment to be made.

You can find information about correct notice and other matters at gov.uk/parental-bereavement-pay-leave/how-to-claim.

How much do you get?

£187.18 a week (or 90 per cent of your average weekly earnings, if less).

How do you claim?

Contact your employer. There is no claim form, but you must give your employer the correct notice and information.

Statutory paternity pay

Statutory paternity pay is paid by employers to certain employees who are taking time off work to care for a child. Your entitlement is not affected by your income or capital. It is paid for up to two weeks.

Who can claim?

You qualify if all of the following apply.

- You are the father, the husband or partner of the mother (or the adopter of the child), the child's adopter or the intended parent if you are having a baby through a surrogacy arrangement.
- You have worked for your employer continuously for at least 26 weeks by the 15th week before the baby is due.
- You are employed by your employer up to the date of birth.
- Your average gross earnings are at least a certain level – £125 a week at the time of writing.
- You give the correct notice to your employer.
- You are in the statutory paternity pay period – this is a maximum of two consecutive weeks. The earliest date that statutory paternity pay can be paid from is the child's date of birth (or the date of their placement for adoption) and the latest is eight weeks after this date.

You can find information about the notice and proof at gov.uk/paternity-pay-leave/how-to-claim.

How much do you get?

£187.18 a week (or 90 per cent of your average weekly earnings, if less).

How do you claim?

Contact your employer. You must give your employer the correct notice. You do not have to use a claim form but you can use Form SC3 to give information and notice to your employer for a birth or Form SC4 for an adoption. They are available from gov.uk/paternity-pay-leave.

Statutory shared parental pay

Statutory shared parental pay is paid by an employer to an employee whose partner has given up her statutory maternity pay, maternity allowance or statutory adoption pay early. The remaining pay can be paid to the mother's partner as statutory shared parental pay to enable both partners to stop work and care for the child. You can be paid for a maximum of 37 weeks.

Who can claim?

You qualify if all of the following apply.

- You are the child's mother or father, or the mother's partner.
- The mother has given up her statutory maternity allowance, maternity allowance or statutory adoption pay early.
- You have worked for your employer continuously for at least 26 weeks by the 15th week before the baby is due (or in adoption cases, the week in which you were notified of being matched with a child).
- Your average gross earnings are at least a certain level – £125 a week at the time of writing.
- Your partner (or if they are not your partner, the other parent or the adopter) has been employed or self-employed for 26 weeks in the 66 weeks up to the week before the baby is due (or in

adoption cases, the week in which the adopter was notified of the match).
- Your partner (or if they are not your partner, the other parent or the adopter) had average earnings of at least £30 a week in 13 weeks out of the above 66-week period.
- You give the correct notice and information to your employer.

You can find information about the notice and proof at gov.uk/shared-parental-leave-and-pay/applying-for-leave-and-pay.

How much do you get?

£187.18 a week (or 90 per cent of your average weekly earnings, if less).

How do you claim?

Contact your employer. There is no claim form, but you must give your employer the correct notice and information.

Sure Start maternity grant

A Sure Start maternity grant is a £500 lump sum payable to people on a low income to help with the costs of a new baby in England and Wales. If you live in Scotland, see the information on Best Start grant.

Who can claim?

You can get a Sure Start maternity grant if you or your partner or dependant is pregnant and within 11 weeks of the expected week of childbirth, or has given birth within the last six months. You can also qualify if you are not the mother or the mother's partner, and you are responsible for a child who is no more than 12 months old – eg, you are the guardian, or through adoption or surrogacy. You must also be getting one of the following qualifying benefits:

- universal credit

- income-related employment and support allowance
- pension credit

If you have another child under 16, you cannot usually get the grant, although there are exceptions.

- If the other child or children in your family are adopted or you are a kinship carer or foster carer, you can get a grant if they were over 12 months old when you became responsible for them.
- If you are a refugee or have humanitarian protection, or are in the UK under schemes for people who fled Afghanistan or Ukraine, you can get a grant for a first baby born in the UK even if you have another child or children born before you came to the UK.
- If you have a multiple birth, you can get a grant, but the number of grants is reduced if you have other children under 16. If you are claiming for your dependant's first child, you can get a grant.

How much do you get?

A Sure Start maternity grant is £500 for each child or expected child.

How do you claim?

Apply for a Sure Start maternity grant by post on Form SF100, downloadable from gov.uk/sure-start-maternity-grant/how-to-claim or sent to you on request by phoning the Sure Start Maternity Grant helpline on 0800 169 0140 (Relay UK dial 18001 first; Welsh language 0800 169 0240; textphone 0800 169 0286; British Sign Language services available).

You are asked to provide evidence of pregnancy or childbirth from a health professional such as your doctor or midwife; either the MAT B1 form or a statement. Don't delay sending the form if you are close to the time limit; you can send the evidence later.

You can claim from 11 weeks before the expected week of childbirth to up to six months after the birth. If you are claiming in other circumstances such as adoption, you can claim up to six months after the date you became responsible for the child, and the child is no more than 12 months old when you claim.

If you are waiting to hear about a claim for universal credit or pension credit, you must still claim within the time limit. If your maternity grant claim is refused, you should reclaim within three months of the qualifying benefit being awarded.

Universal credit

Universal credit is a benefit paid by the DWP to working-age people who are on a low income. Your entitlement is affected by your income and capital, but you do not need to have paid national insurance contributions. Universal credit can be paid to you whether you are in or out of work, and whether or not you are able to work. You can get it as a lone parent or a couple, carer or disabled person.

Who can claim?

You qualify if all of the following conditions are met.

- You are at least 18, but under pension age. Some 16/17-year-olds who have a child or are pregnant can also claim.
- You are not receiving education. Some exceptions apply, including if you have a child or are a foster parent, or your partner is not receiving education.
- You satisfy the habitual residence test and the right to reside test, and you are not a person subject to immigration control.
- You have accepted a claimant commitment.
- You do not have £16,000 or more in capital, and your income is low enough.

If you are a member of a couple, you make a joint claim and usually your partner must also satisfy the above conditions, although there are exceptions, including where your partner has reached pension age.

How much do you get?

The amount of universal credit depends on your circumstances and income. There is a standard allowance for adults, either as a single person or a couple, but lower amounts if you (and your partner, if you are claiming as a couple) are under 25. There are additional amounts if you or your partner have been assessed as having limited capability for work and work-related activity, or are a carer.

If you pay rent, or service charges in some cases, a housing costs element is included, although this might not cover your rent in full if you are in private rented accommodation or if you are in local authority or housing association accommodation and have a spare bedroom.

A child element is included for children. However, the two-child limit means an amount cannot be included for a third or subsequent child born on or after 6 April 2017, unless one of the following applies.

- The child was the second or subsequent child in a multiple birth.
- The child is living with you because they are unable to live with their parents and either there is a child arrangements order, you are their legal guardian or kinship carer, or it is likely that the child would have to go into local authority care if they were not living with you.
- The child has been placed with you for adoption or formally adopted by you in the UK.
- It is likely that the child was born as the result of rape, or in a controlling or coercive relationship, and you are not living with the perpetrator.
- The child's parent is a child aged under 16 for whom you are responsible.

An additional amount is included for a disabled child, even if you cannot get a basic child element for that child due to the two-child limit. You can also get an amount included for the cost of your childcare if you are in work (if you are claiming as a couple, your partner must also be in work, unless they are a carer or have limited capability for work).

The amount you get depends on your and your partner's income in each monthly assessment period.

The total you can receive may be limited by the benefit cap, but this does not apply if you, your partner or child receive a disability or carer's benefit, or are earning over a certain level.

If you have moved from legacy benefits to universal credit, you may be getting a transitional element, intended to make up for a loss of income. However, this transitional element is reduced when other universal credit elements increase or new elements are added, so you may find that the amount you receive remains the same for some time.

How do you claim?

Universal credit must usually be claimed online. There is no paper claim form. To start your claim, go to gov.uk/apply-universal-credit.

If you need help claiming online, contact the helpline on 0800 328 5644 (Relay UK dial 18001 first; Welsh language 0800 328 1744; textphone 0800 328 1344; British Sign Language services available). You can also get help making a claim from the Citizens Advice 'Help to Claim' service.

If you cannot claim online, the DWP may accept a claim by phone.

You need to be able to check your online account regularly, ideally daily, or you might miss important instructions and could lose benefit. You must set up an email account if you do not have one. Ask for help at your local job centre if you are not confident you can manage online.

Winter fuel payment

Winter fuel payment is a lump-sum payment to help pay fuel bills in England and Wales. You must be at least pension age to qualify.

It is payable per household at either £200 if you are under 80, or £300 if you are 80 or over. If your individual annual income is over £35,000, winter fuel payment will be recovered through income tax.

Winter fuel payment is paid automatically.

Winter heating payments (in Scotland)

There are three different payments to help with winter heating costs in Scotland:

- winter heating payment for low income households with young children, disabilities or older people
- child winter heating payment for severely disabled children
- pension age winter heating payment for older people in Scotland

Who can qualify?

There are different ways to qualify for the different payments, and you may qualify for more than one.

- Winter heating payment is payable if you get:
  - universal credit with a disabled child element (regardless of earnings)
  - universal credit if you have a child under five or limited capability for work, and you have no earnings
  - pension credit
- Child winter heating payment is payable for a child who is entitled to the highest rate of the care component of child disability payment, or the enhanced rate of the daily living component of adult disability payment (regardless of other income).
- Pension age winter heating payment is payable if you are over pension age.

How much do you get?

Winter heating payment is a one-off payment of £59.75 made between December and February.

Child winter heating payment is a one-off payment of £255.80 for each child who qualifies, made by the end of December.

Pension age winter heating payment is payable per household at either £203.40 if you are under 80, or £305.10 if you are 80 or over. If your individual annual income is over £35,000, the payment will be recovered through income tax.

How do you claim?

You do not need to claim any of the winter heating payments. If you meet the conditions, they should be paid automatically into the account nominated for the qualifying benefit or state pension. If you think you qualify and have not received a payment, contact Social Security Scotland on 0800 182 2222.

Young carer grant

Young carer grants are paid by Social Security Scotland to young people aged 16 to 18 living in Scotland who care for someone with a disability.

Who can claim?

You qualify if all of the following apply.

- You live in Scotland.
- You are aged at least 16 and under 19.
- You are caring (usually for an average of at least 16 hours a week) for a person who is receiving any of the following:
  - attendance allowance or pension age disability payment
  - either the highest or the middle rate of disability living allowance or child disability payment care component
  - either rate of the daily living component of personal independence payment or adult disability payment
  - armed forces independence payment
  - constant attendance allowance with an industrial injury benefit or war pension

- You are not entitled to carer's allowance or carer support payment.

How much do you get?

£390.25 paid as an annual payment.

How do you claim?

Claim on the form (online or downloadable) at mygov.scot/young-carer-grant/how-to-apply, by phoning Social Security Scotland on 0800 182 2222 or, if you use British Sign Language, via Contact Scotland BSL.

Appendix

Glossary of terms

Advance
An advance payment of universal credit that you can get if you are in hardship while waiting for a universal credit payment.

Alternative payment arrangements
The discretion to pay universal credit twice a month, directly to a landlord or split between partners.

Appointee
Someone, often a relative, authorised by the DWP or Social Security Scotland to claim and receive benefit on another person's behalf if that person is either under 16 or cannot claim for themselves – eg, because of a learning disability.

Assessment period
The monthly period on which payment of universal credit is based. You are paid up to seven days after the end of each assessment period.

Bedroom tax
A reduction in the amount of the housing costs element in universal credit, affecting tenants of local authorities and housing associations who have one or more spare bedroom.

Benefit cap
The maximum amount of working-age social security benefits that someone can receive. It includes universal credit, child benefit and some other benefits, but there are some exceptions and some people to whom the cap does not apply.

Budgeting advance
A discretionary extra amount of universal credit to help with expenses, paid as a loan. You must usually have been on universal credit for at least six months to qualify.

Capital
This includes savings, investments, certain lump-sum payments and property which is not a person's main home.

Care component
The part of disability living allowance or child disability payment (in Scotland) paid for help with bodily functions or supervision.

Carer element
An extra amount in universal credit (or a pension credit carer amount) paid to people who care for a disabled child or adult.

Child element
An extra amount for children included in a person's maximum universal credit (or a pension credit child amount).

Childcare element
An extra amount in universal credit paid to people in work who pay for childcare.

Claimant commitment
An agreement setting out what you must do while claiming universal credit, and the possible penalties if its terms are not met.

Collect and pay
When the Child Maintenance Service collects money from the child's other parent and then pays you.

Connected person carer
A person who has taken responsibility for the child of a friend or relative under a formal caring arrangement, or an informal caring arrangement where it is likely the child would otherwise be looked after by the local authority. Sometimes referred to as a kinship carer or a friend and family carer.

Contributory benefit
A benefit that requires the claimant to have paid, or been credited with, national insurance contributions in order to be entitled to it.

Daily living component

The part of personal independence payment or adult disability payment (in Scotland) paid if you have problems with daily living activities, or are terminally ill.

Determination

The term used by Social Security Scotland for a decision.

Disabled child addition

An extra amount of universal credit (or pension credit) paid for a child or young person who gets disability living allowance, personal independence payment or child disability payment (in Scotland), or who is blind.

Discretionary housing payment

A payment that can be made by a local authority to top up universal credit or housing benefit when someone in rented accommodation needs extra help with their housing costs.

Domestic abuse

Any incident or pattern of physical, financial, psychological, emotional or sexual abuse, including controlling, coercive or threatening behaviour, perpetrated by a partner, ex-partner, close relative or carer.

Earnings threshold

The amount of a person's earnings (or joint earnings for couples) above which there is no expectation to look for more work, or meet any other work-related requirements for universal credit.

Elements

Amounts for children, disabilities, caring responsibilities, housing and childcare, which make up part of a person's maximum universal credit award.

Family-based arrangement

An agreement made between the parents of a child rather than through the Child Maintenance Service or the courts.

Flexible Support Fund

A discretionary fund to help remove barriers to work, administered by local job centres.

Friend and family carer
A person who has taken responsibility for the child of a friend or relative under a formal caring arrangement, or an informal caring arrangement where it is likely the child would otherwise be looked after by the local authority. Sometimes referred to as a connected person carer or a kinship carer.

Grace period
A nine-month period when the benefit cap does not apply to your universal credit because your earnings in the last year were above a certain amount.

Guarantee credit
A type of pension credit for people whose income is below a certain level.

Habitual residence test
A test of whether someone has a settled intention to stay in the UK for the time being (or Republic of Ireland, Channel Islands or Isle of Man; for Best Start grant and young carer grant the UK, Channel Islands, Isle of Man or European Economic Area), who has usually been living here for a period. For some benefits, a right to reside is also required to pass the test.

Hardship payments
Reduced-rate payments of universal credit that you can apply for if your benefit has been reduced due to a sanction or benefit offence.

Healthcare professional
A doctor, nurse, paramedic, physiotherapist or occupational therapist who carries out assessments for disability benefits.

Housing costs element
The amount of universal credit that helps with rent and certain service charges.

Independent Case Examiner
A body handling complaints about the DWP.

Interim payment
An amount of housing benefit or child benefit that may be paid when there is a delay in paying someone their full entitlement.

Jobseeking conditions
What you must do to be ready for work and to look for work in order to get jobseeker's allowance.

Kinship carer
A person who has taken responsibility for the child of a friend, relative or someone they know. This may be a formal or informal arrangement. Sometimes the child is looked after by the local authority. Sometimes referred to as a connected person carer or a friend and family carer.

Limited capability for work
A test of whether a person's ability to work is limited by a health condition.

Limited capability for work element
There is generally no extra amount of money in new claims of universal credit for people found to have limited capability for work. But some people on universal credit are entitled to the limited capability for work element – eg, if they transfer to universal credit from employment and support allowance with an entitlement to extra money for being in the work-related activity group.

Limited capability for work-related activity
A test of how severe a person's health problems are and whether their ability to prepare for work is limited.

Limited capability for work-related activity element
An extra amount of universal credit paid to people who are too ill to prepare for work or who have a severe disability.

Local housing allowance
The maximum amount of help with your rent if you live in private rented accommodation. The amount depends on how many bedrooms you need and the broad rental market area you live in.

Local welfare assistance schemes
Run by local authorities to help people in need – eg, in a crisis or to ease exceptional pressure on a family.

Looked after
Describes a child in the formal care of the local authority under certain legal provisions. A looked after child might be placed with foster carers, kinship carers or in residential accommodation of some kind. A child who is looked after by the local authority may be living at home in some circumstances, in which case they are still treated as a member of the family.

Main carer
The person in a couple who spends the most time looking after the children, jointly nominated by the couple.

Mandatory reconsideration
The requirement to have a decision looked at again before an appeal can be made.

Mandatory reconsideration notice
The notice sent by the DWP after someone makes a mandatory reconsideration request, which is needed in order to appeal.

Means-tested benefit
A benefit that is only paid if your income and capital are low enough, and which also considers the circumstances of your partner.

Mobility component
The part of disability living allowance or personal independence payment (or, in Scotland, adult disability payment or child disability payment) paid if you have mobility problems.

National minimum wage
A set minimum hourly rate that employers must pay. The government calls the rate for people aged 21 or over the national living wage.

No recourse to public funds
Describes people without the required immigration status that enables them to claim public funds. Public funds are defined in the Immigration Rules at gov.uk/guidance/immigration-rules/immigration-rules-introduction.

Non-advanced education
Education below degree and diploma level, including national vocational qualification levels 1–3, GCSEs, A levels and Scottish Highers.

Non-dependant
An adult, other than a partner, who lives with the person claiming benefit – eg, a grown-up daughter or son, relative or friend.

Overpayment
An amount of benefit that is paid to you, which is more than your entitlement and which you may be asked to repay.

Pension age
The earliest age you can claim a state pension.

Person subject to immigration control
Someone who requires leave to enter or remain in the UK but does not have it, or who has leave to remain but is prohibited from having recourse to public funds, or has leave to remain in the UK on the basis of a sponsorship agreement.

Pre-settled status
Limited leave to remain granted under the European Union Settlement Scheme to European Economic Area nationals, their family members and those with derivative residence rights who have lived in the UK for less than five years.

Qualifying child
A child who is under 16 or under 20 and in full-time, non-advanced education and for whom you can get child maintenance.

Real-time information
A system whereby employers send HM Revenue and Customs information about employees' earnings every time they are paid, which is then used by the DWP to adjust universal credit awards.

Redetermination
The requirement for Social Security Scotland benefits to have a decision looked at again before an appeal can be made.

Referral
When you contact the advice service and start the process of making an appointment, you have made a referral.

Right to reside test
A social security test, mainly affecting European Economic Area nationals, which must be satisfied in order to claim certain benefits.

Sanction
A reduction in a person's benefit award for failing to meet certain work-related requirements.

Settled status
Defined in immigration law as being ordinarily resident in the UK without any restrictions on the time the person is able to remain here. Generally used to refer to those with indefinite leave, including when granted under the European Union Settlement Scheme.

Short-term advance
An advance of benefit which can be paid if someone is in hardship while waiting for their first benefit payment, and sometimes in other circumstances.

Signpost
When you give your client details of an advice service, for them to get in touch with the service directly.

Social Security Scotland
Agency which delivers social security benefits that are devolved to Scottish government.

Standard allowance
The basic amount of universal credit paid for a single adult or a couple.

Support component
An amount included in employment and support allowance for people who have limited capability for work-related activity.

Support group
Refers to people the DWP has assessed as having limited capability for work-related activity.

Tax-free childcare
A UK-wide scheme that helps working parents pay for childcare. For every £8 a parent pays, the government pays an extra £2 towards childcare costs, up to £2,000 per child, a year (or £4,000 for children who are disabled).

Terminal illness
A progressive disease from which your death can reasonably be expected within 12 months. For Scottish benefits, the definition does not include any timescale within which death is expected.

Two-child limit
A restriction on the number of child elements included in universal credit, relating to children born on or after 6 April 2017. There are exceptions – for example, if a child is adopted or for multiple births.

Variation
The process that enables someone to apply to the Child Maintenance Service to more accurately assess the income or circumstances of the paying parent.

Work allowance
The amount of earnings families and people who are ill or disabled are allowed to keep before their universal credit is affected.

Work availability
One of the work-related requirements, which means being willing and able to take up paid work, usually within 90 minutes' travel time of home.

Work capability assessment
A social security test used to decide whether someone is too ill to work.

Work coach
Someone employed by the DWP to draw up claimant commitments, update them and check that people are meeting their work-related requirements.

Work-focused interview
A compulsory interview with the DWP to discuss job opportunities, barriers to work and training.

Work preparation
One of the work-related requirements, which includes carrying out activities to prepare for a future return to work, such as increasing skills or doing a work placement.

Work-related activity
Activity that makes it more likely that someone will get a job or remain in work.

Work-related activity component
An amount included in employment and support allowance for people who have limited capability for work and whose claim started before 6 April 2017.

Work-related requirements
The activities that a person must undertake to continue to receive the full amount of universal credit.

Work search
One of the work-related requirements, which means normally spending 35 hours a week (expected hours) looking for work. Your expected hours are 30 hours a week if you have a child under 13, or may be lower due to health issues or caring responsibilities.

Index